THE

PUBLICATIONS

OF THE

Northamptonshire Record Society

FOUNDED IN DECEMBER, 1920

VOLUME XXVII

FOR THE YEAR ENDED 31 DECEMBER 1974

LORD CHANCELLOR
HATTON 1589

TANDEM SI

SIR CHRISTOPHER HATTON

NORTHAMPTONSHIRE LIEUTENANCY PAPERS

AND OTHER DOCUMENTS 1580-1614

EDITED BY

JEREMY GORING

AND

JOAN WAKE

Printed for
The Northamptonshire Record Society
by Northumberland Press Ltd.
Gateshead
1975

© Northamptonshire Record Society 1975

ISBN 0 901275 34 4

PRINTED IN GREAT BRITAIN

CONTENTS

ILLUSTRATIONS

GENERAL EDITOR'S PREFACE

This volume is the last of five texts edited by Miss Joan Wake, a founder of the Northamptonshire Record Society and its General Editor until 1965, who died in January 1974. It is one of two editions on which Miss Wake was actively engaged in the 1960s; the other was *The Letters of Daniel Eaton*, published by the Society in 1971.

The names of two editors appear on the title-page of this edition; but they have worked consecutively not concurrently on it. In 1972 Miss Wake handed over responsibility for the edition to Dr. Jeremy Goring of Goldsmiths' College, London. The division of work has been as follows. The text was established by Miss Wake, and was in galley proof when Dr. Goring took over. Dr. Goring has revised the text and editorial matter, selected documents for the appendices, and written a full introduction to the text.

E.J.K.

ACKNOWLEDGMENTS

Had Miss Wake lived to see the publication of this volume she would doubtless have wished to record her gratitude to those who, over the years, had eased her editorial burdens: to Miss Frances Page, Miss Elliott Lockhart, Mr. Patrick King, Chief Archivist of the Northamptonshire Record Office, and probably to many others. She would also, I am sure, have wished to acknowledge the helpfulness and forbearance of the manager and staff of the Northumberland Press.

For my part I should like to record my indebtedness to those who, in varying ways, have helped to lighten my load: to Mr. King and the Northamptonshire Archives Committee, who gave me the exclusive use of the "Hatton book" for the best part of a year, and to the Trustees of the British Museum, who agreed to its temporary deposit among their MSS; to Dr. Edmund King, the General Editor, who performed the role of "middleman" with exemplary patience and good humour; to the members of Professor S. T. Bindoff's seminar at the Institute of Historical Research, London, who endured two readings of the draft Introduction and made valuable comments and criticisms; and, last but not least, to my children, Charles, George, Margaret and Daniel, whose cheerful assistance with the preparation of the index removed much of the tedium from that normally joyless task.

JEREMY GORING

NOTE ON EDITORIAL METHOD

With the exception of Hatton's original Commission of Lieutenancy, which it was deemed appropriate to print first even though it is not the earliest item, the documents in this collection have been re-arranged in approximate chronological order; as a rule, however, enclosures have been placed irrespective of date immediately after the letters that enclosed them. Original spelling has been retained throughout, abbreviations have normally been extended where possible, punctuation has been modernised and initial capital letters have been rationalised. Original signatures have been placed between inverted commas, except in the case of holograph letters.

ABBREVIATIONS

A.P.C.	*Acts of the Privy Council of England* (New Series).
Eoynton	L. Boynton, *The Elizabethan Militia, 1558-1638* (1967).
Brooks	E. St. J. Brooks, *Sir Christopher Hatton* (1946).
Cruickshank	C. G. Cruickshank, *Elizabeth's Army* (2nd. edn., Oxford, 1966)
D.N.B.	*Dictionary of National Biography.*
H.M.C.	Historical Manuscripts Commission.
M.B.S.	*Musters, Beacons, Subsidies, etc. in the County of Northampton, 1586-1623*, ed. Joan Wake (Northants Rec. Soc. iii, 1926).
M.M.B.	*The Montagu Musters Book, 1602-1623*, ed. Joan Wake (Northants Rec. Soc. vii, 1935).
P.R.O.	Public Record Office, London.
Scott Thomson	Gladys Scott Thomson, *Lords Lieutenants in the Sixteenth Century* (1923).

SIGNS IN THE TEXT

[ ]	*Word(s) or letter(s) lost or illegible—or omitted in error by the writer of the document—and supplied conjecturally by the editor.*
[ᵈ]	*Words written in error and subsequently deleted.*
[ⁱ]	*Words inserted, either between the lines or in the margin.*

INTRODUCTION

When in 1869 representatives of the newly-established Historical Manuscripts Commission visited Haverholme Priory in Lincolnshire, the seat of George Finch-Hatton, Earl of Winchilsea and Nottingham, they discovered among his archives "a book of Northampton Papers, concerning the County Militia, 1588".[1] Apart from this brief description, taken almost verbatim from the title on the volume's spine, their report contained no further information; and it was not until the early 1920s, when Miss Joan Wake was given permission to consult it, that the book's contents were finally revealed.[2] It immediately became apparent that there was a close relationship between these "Hatton" papers and those in Sir Richard Knightley's book, which Miss Wake was then editing for publication under the title of *Musters, Beacons, Subsidies*. In his introduction to the edition Dr. John E. Morris made extensive use of the documents in the "Hatton book", which, he surmised, had been put together at Holdenby during the period when Sir Christopher Hatton was lord lieutenant of Northamptonshire and had later passed, with other Hatton MSS., to Kirby Hall and subsequently to Haverholme Priory.[3] From this the impression arose that the volume was Hatton's own "lieutenancy book"—the only known example of a systematic collection of militia papers made by a lord lieutenant before the seventeenth century.

There are, however, reasons for thinking that this interpretation is mistaken. To begin with, as Morris was well aware, the book contains some documents relating to militia matters which do not belong to the period of Hatton's lieutenancy, and others which, although they date from the period 1586 to 1591 and do concern Hatton, do not relate to the lieutenancy. Again there are a few documents which have nothing to do with the lieutenancy or with Hatton and almost certainly never passed through his hands. But it is to be doubted if even those items that do relate directly to Hatton's lieutenancy (and these admittedly constitute the majority of the documents in the book) could ever have formed part of a collection of papers at Holdenby or indeed at any of Sir Christopher's other houses. Morris argued that the *raison d'être* of the "Hatton book" was the lord lieutenant's custom of requiring his deputies to take copies of all communications received from him and then to return the originals to Holdenby. He was led to this conclusion by the discovery of a request by Hatton to his deputies to make a copy of one particular document—his renewed commission of 1588—and then "with all conuenient speede to returne the same unto me" (**52**). He apparently did not notice that, as Hatton was then at Greenwich, there was no question of the document being "returned to Holdenby". Hatton in fact was hardly ever at Holdenby;

[1] H.M.C. 1st Rep., p. 32.
[2] *M.B.S.*, p. xxii.
[3] *Ibid.*, pp. lii-liii.

only one letter (7) in the present collection was written there. He also seems to have been unaware that the occasion to which he refers was the *only* one on which Sir Christopher is known to have asked his correspondents to return a document; he made the request on this occasion because, having no time to prepare the customary "transumpt" of his commission, he had rashly sent his deputies the original—which naturally he wanted back. To have required them to return every communication that he sent them would have been, to say the least, most unusual; a more obvious procedure would have been that adopted by some seventeenth century lord lieutenants, who kept copies of all the letters that they sent out.[1] Moreover, were the "Hatton book" a genuine lieutenancy book of this kind, it would have contained a record not only of his letters to his deputies but also of their letters to him. Two such letters do in fact survive, but they are not in the present collection; they are among the state papers preserved in the Public Record Office.[2]

If then this is not, as Morris averred, a collection of papers sent out to Hatton's deputies and later "returned to Holdenby and bound up in the Hatton book", what can it be? Whose papers were they? At first sight the most likely original owner of the papers would seem to be Sir Richard Knightley, Hatton's deputy-lieutenant and trusted friend. With only two exceptions (96, 98) all the documents in the collection date from periods in which he was actively involved in the administration of the shire—as justice of the peace, muster commissioner or deputy-lieutenant. Significantly there are no documents dating from the second half of 1589 or the first half of 1590, when this zealous puritan gentleman was in disgrace and excluded from public life owing to his involvement in the affair of the Marprelate Tracts.[3] A large proportion of the documents are in fact letters addressed to Knightley either individually or in association with others. One of the individual letters (93) touches upon a purely personal matter and has nothing to do with the militia or any aspect of local administration. Most of the other letters were ones addressed to him jointly with his fellow-deputy Sir Edward Montagu; and since Montagu often seems to have received them first[4] and then sent them on to his colleague, it is likely that they ended up in Knightley's keeping.[5] On the other hand it could be argued that, since a considerable number of the documents are also found—either in their entirety or in abbreviated form —in Knightley's own militia book,[6] he himself did not retain them permanently. Most people, it might be imagined, would not have gone to the trouble of having copies made of documents that they intended to keep. But then Knightley was not like most people; he seems to have been exceptionally efficient and business-like. Fearing that a bundle of

---

[1] See, e.g., *The Earl of Hertford's Lieutenancy Papers, 1603-1612*, ed. W. P. D. Murphy (Wiltshire Rec. Soc., xxiii, 1969).

[2] See Appendix 2 and 3.

[3] For Knightley's career, see the accounts in *D.N.B.* (which contains some errors) and in *M.B.S.*, p. xxi. His imprisonment lasted from early in November 1589 until some date after his trial on 13 Feb. 1590: W. Pierce, *An Historical Introduction to the Marprelate Tracts* (1908), pp. 205-7, 319.

[4] See, e.g. 46 and 51.

[5] For the much smaller number of militia papers for the years 1580-91 that ended up in Montagu's keeping, see H.M.C. *Buccleuch*, iii. 18-29 and H.M.C. *Montagu of Beaulieu*, pp. 12ff.

[6] See *M.B.S.*, pp. 1-23.

loose papers might easily get lost or destroyed, he may well have decided to keep a careful record of the more important items in a special book. There appears therefore to be no insuperable objection to the theory that the great bulk of the documents in this collection[1]—93 out of a total of 98—were once in Knightley's possession and remained there, perhaps to the end of his life.

There are, however, five items that almost certainly did not form part of Knightley's permanent collection: a letter from the privy council to Bartholomew Tate (**26**), with an enclosure (**25**); and one from Sir Euseby Andrew to Sir William Tate (**96**), with two enclosures (**97, 98**). The presence in this collection of the last three items, which belong to the reign of James I, has been regarded as "a mystery";[2] but it does in fact provide a clue to the circumstances in which the collection came together. The documents date from 1613 and 1614, which were years of crisis in England; after a long period of peace there were revived fears of a Spanish invasion and much anxious thought was given to the problem of strengthening the local militia. In Northamptonshire Sir William Tate was gradually taking over from the aged Knightley the oversight of the western division of the county. Faced with the unfamiliar task of making preparations to resist invasion he may have sought his older colleague's advice as to how he should proceed. He may also have asked for the loan of any documents in Knightley's keeping which might throw light upon how things had been arranged in earlier years. This is no fanciful suggestion; at this period, it has been suggested, collections of militia papers "acquired the authority of reference-books" and were much in demand as "models" of administrative procedure.[3] In this way Knightley's collection of militia papers, bundled up with other documents from the Armada period, may have passed to Tate; indeed Sir Euseby Andrew, who was Tate's cousin and Knightley's son-in-law, and was evidently acting as an intermediary between the two men in 1614, may have effected the transfer. If this surmise is accurate it is possible that at the time of Knightley's death in 1615 Tate had possession of all the documents in the "Hatton book": the 93 "Knightley" items, the three Jacobean documents and the two letters that had belonged to his father, Bartholomew Tate. But the question remains: Who was responsible for putting them together into the volume which eventually found its way into the Hatton library at Kirby Hall?

The most likely person is Sir William Tate's younger brother Francis, founder member and former secretary of the Society of Antiquaries and an avid collector of manuscripts. Unlike many contemporary collectors he was interested not only in "antiquities" but also in more recent history; for instance, he made a collection of "Learned speeches in Parliaments held in the latter end of Queen Elizabeth and in the reign of King James I". Furthermore, he made a study of the history of his native Northamptonshire and provided Augustine Vincent with material for his projected survey of the shire.[4] He may well have had a particular interest in documents relating to the career of Sir Christopher Hatton, a great

---

[1] Including some miscellaneous items, such as **23**, **36**, and **49**, which *could* have belonged to Knightley, although this cannot be proved.
[2] *M.B.S.*, p. cxxii.
[3] Boynton, p. 49.
[4] D.N.B. s.v. Francis Tate.

parliamentarian and a famous son of Northamptonshire who also happened to have been his father's first cousin and especial friend.[1] If it was Francis Tate who brought together the present collection of papers, it is not surprising that the volume came into the possession of the Hatton family; for it was in Lord Hatton's library at Kirby Hall that later in the century two of the antiquary's MS. volumes were said to have been "reserved as rarities".[2] Moreover, if this collection of documents did have its origin in the Tate family house near Northampton, it is singularly appropriate that more than three centuries later it should have come back to Delapré to lie among the archives of the Northamptonshire Record Office. But whoever it was who preserved the collection deserves the gratitude of historians, for it provides some vivid illustrations of the problems of county administration in England in the later Elizabethan period.

County Administration

In Northamptonshire, as in every other shire in the realm, the major responsibility for local administration was borne by the leading local families who constituted the effective membership of the commission of the peace. As a rule it was a responsibility which they bore gladly; for although the work was often onerous and invariably unpaid,[3] it was considered an honour to be appointed to the commission and a great disgrace to be removed from it.[4] The number of J.P.s varied according to the size of the shire; it was usually thought desirable for there to be at least one to every hundred.[5] In the twenty hundreds into which Northamptonshire was divided there were at this period about thirty resident J.P.s; this suggests that the coverage was adequate, although it appears that there were a number of hundreds in both the eastern and western divisions of the shire which lacked a resident J.P.[6] The total number of J.P.s in Northamptonshire, as elsewhere, had been growing since the beginning of the century, partly because, owing to the increase in the number of gentry, there were more aspirants for office, and partly because, owing to the increasing complexity of local administration, there were more duties to be performed. The magistrates' duties were multifarious. Under the general supervision of the privy council it was their task to administer justice, enforce economic regulations, supervise poor relief,[7] raise taxes, maintain religious uniformity, control the militia and ensure that in every respect the laws of the land were obeyed.

Among these multifarious tasks perhaps the most tedious and

[1] Brooks, pp. 78-80, 158-59.
[2] A. à Wood, *Athenae Oxoniensis* (1815), ii. 179.
[3] A small allowance was in fact paid for attendance at Quarter Sessions.
[4] The Crown used the threat of dismissal as a device for disciplining negligent J.P.s; see **33**, clause 41.
[5] See **33**, clause 27.
[6] A list of Northamptonshire J.P.s for 1584 is printed in J. H. Gleason, *The Justices of the Peace in England, 1558 to 1640* (Oxford, 1969), pp. 167-68. For the names and locations of the hundreds, ten of which were in the eastern division of the shire and ten in the western, see the map on p. xv. For the hundred of Nassaburgh, which enjoyed a measure of independence from the shire, see *M.B.S.*, p. xvii note.
[7] See **33**, clauses 32 and 33.

THE NORTHAMPTONSHIRE HUNDREDS
showing the boundary between the
East and West divisions

unexciting was the enforcement of economic regulations. In the sixteenth
century, as in our own day, Englishmen were much troubled by rising
prices, and the J.P.s were continually being called upon to regulate them;
there was little that they could do about the long-term upward trend, but
they could at least try to do something about the short-term rises caused
by temporary food shortages. In February 1591, in an attempt to deal with
the shortage of meat occasioned by the death of many sheep and "other
cattell" in the previous year's drought, the local authorities were ordered
to take special care over the enforcement of restrictions on the eating of
meat in Lent (94, 95).[1] The illegal eating of meat in Lent and on the
weekly "fish-days" may have been a particularly common practice in
Northamptonshire, where meat was plentiful and fresh fish presumably
scarce; and it is therefore doubtful whether the deputy-lieutenants, who
probably disliked salt fish as much as anyone, had much success in

---

[1] The restrictions on meat-eating in Lent and on "other usual fasting days" were
primarily intended to encourage the fishing industry and thus maintain the navy.

enforcing the privy council's edict. Shortages of meat, however, presented a less serious problem than shortages of corn. In 1586 and 1587 there was a universal dearth of grain owing to the "vnseasonablenes of theis latter yeares" (**31**), and magistrates throughout England were ordered to take action against "badgers", "ingrossers" and "purveyers", whose wholesale purchases of corn were thought to have contributed to the shortage (**33**). The activities of purveyors, who claimed the right to buy corn and other victuals for the royal household at fixed prices, were in fact a continual cause of trouble at this time, and in 1588 the Earl of Leicester, as Lord Steward, was appointed to undertake an enquiry into their malpractices (**49**). Technically, it seems, these men had no right to operate in Northamptonshire, for the J.P.s there had long since agreed to compound for purveyance and had undertaken to levy special taxes instead, but the shire was probably still being plagued by them.[1] Be that as it may, there is no doubt that the inhabitants did suffer from the activities of those other Tudor bogeymen, the "forestallers" and "regrators", who bought corn direct from the growers and so by-passed the common markets (**27**).

In Northamptonshire, as in some other Midland shires, the enforcement of regulations against forestallers and regrators—or those prohibiting the feeding of "graine" to sheep (**26**)—must have been an almost impossible task, since the economy of the shire was geared to supplying corn and meat to distant markets. There was also a particular problem in the town of Northampton, where corn was in short supply not merely because it was being carted away for sale elsewhere but because increasing quantities were being consumed by the malt kilns. In November 1586 the inhabitants of the town (among them John Hatton, a humble cousin of Sir Christopher), complaining that they were "not able to maynteyne oure wyves, children and famelies with nedefull bread", asked Hatton and Mildmay (the two privy councillors whom they thought would be most sympathetic) to take action against the maltsters (**28**). The petition would not have come as a surprise. The problem of the Northampton maltsters, whose expanding activities threatened the town not only with starvation but also with destruction by fire, had vexed the privy council since 1575.[2] Once again the J.P.s were ordered to investigate the matter and deal with the chief offendors, including John Mercer and John Hainsworth (**30**), who had been summoned before the privy council in 1577 for their disobedience to earlier regulations.[3] That the authorities should have taken such pains over this affair is no testimony to their humanitarianism; the matter concerned them because it represented a potential threat to the peace of the realm. What probably moved them to swift action was not so much the "pyttifull teares" of the petitioners as the solemn warning given by the mayor and his brethren: "Our poore people are so hardlie distressed that we stand in great dowte [i.e. fear] of some mutenie or vnlawfull attempte to aryse amongeste them" (**25**). As the terms of Hatton's commission of lieutenancy indicate, the Tudors had an obsessive fear of "ryottes, routes or vnlawfull assemblies" (**1**).

---

[1] See A. Woodworth, "Purveyance for the Royal Household in the reign of Queen Elizabeth", *Trans. Amer. Phil. Soc.*, n.s., pt. 1 (Philadelphia, 1945), pp. 40-41, 46, 77-78.
[2] *A.P.C.*, ix. 8, 345.
[3] *Ibid.*, x. 31, 33, 46-47, 106.

It was this same fear of civil disturbance which coloured the attitude of the authorities to religious dissidents. Elizabethan Northamptonshire was strongly infected with puritanism, often of such a radical nature that its adherents were driven into virtual separation from the established Church.[1] In an age when religious nonconformity was regarded as being politically subversive this presented serious problems to those responsible for the maintenance of order and harmony in the countryside. It was especially serious in a shire where a number of the leading families, such as the Knightleys and the Yelvertons, were themselves strongly puritan in their sympathies. But in the 1580s, although the godly preachers and their gentle patrons were more militant than ever and Northamptonshire was reported to be swarming with "sectaries",[2] the major threat came from a very different group of dissenters. These were the Catholic recusants, those "badd members" of society who "most obstinatly haue refused to come to the Church to prayer and deuine seruice" (51). Among these recusants were some of the most substantial families in Northamptonshire; a list sent to the privy council in May 1586 was headed by the names of William, Lord Vaux of Harrowden and Sir Thomas Tresham.[3] At this time recusants were being looked upon with greater suspicion than heretofore because they were thought to be harbouring "those bloody priests and false traitors"[4] who were entering the country in increasing numbers from the continent. One such was John Ballard, who in 1586 conspired with Anthony Babington to assassinate the Queen; alleged supporters were three members of the Northamptonshire branch of the Arden family, whom Knightley and his godly associate from Oxfordshire, Anthony Cope, were responsible for apprehending in January 1587 (34, 35). But the major consequence of the Babington plot was the removal into the county of Mary, Queen of Scots; at her trial at Fotheringhay in October 1586 Hatton acted as one of the royal commissioners (23), and at her execution there in the following February Knightley and Montagu were present in their capacity as deputy-lieutenants of the shire (36).

At this time, however, a more formidable task assigned to the two deputies was that of rounding up local recusants and committing "the most obstinat and noted persons" among them to prison. The reason for this operation was the belief that Catholics constituted a dangerous "fifth column", able and willing to assist the Spaniards who were known to be preparing to invade the realm (51). Knightley and Montagu were rather dilatory in their performance of this task, ostensibly because they lacked proper instructions (50), but more likely because they, in common with most Englishmen at the time, had no serious doubts about the loyalty of their Catholic neighbours. Apart from that they had more urgent work to do; since the previous autumn, when the lieutenancy had been re-established and orders had come down for the raising of troops on a hitherto unprecedented scale, they and the rest of the Northamptonshire gentry had been obliged to give priority to the task of strengthening the county militia.

[1] See P. Collinson, *The Elizabethan Puritan Movement* (1967), pp. 141-45.
[2] See Hatton's speech at the trial of Sir Richard Knightley (for his complicity in the Marprelate affair) in February 1590; Brooks, p. 338.
[3] P.R.O. SP 12/189/47.
[4] The words were those of Hatton in his famous speech at the opening of Parliament on 4 Feb. 1589: J. E. Neale, *Elizabeth 1 and her Parliaments*, ii (1957), p. 199.

The Northamptonshire Militia

After 1570, when William Parr, Marquess of Northampton ceased to be lord lieutenant of the shire, the control of the Northamptonshire militia was in the hands of muster commissioners drawn from the ranks of the leading gentry. From 1580 onwards there were seven of them: Lord Mordaunt, Sir Walter Mildmay, Sir Thomas Cecil, Sir William Fitzwilliam, Sir John Spencer, Sir Richard Knightley and Sir Edward Montagu, any two of whom had power to act on behalf of them all.[1] Since only the last three were permanently resident in the shire it was inevitable that the main burden fell upon them. Little was changed therefore by the establishment of the lieutenancy in September 1586, when Spencer, Knightley and Montagu were appointed deputy-lieutenants. The main change came on Spencer's death later that year, after which the other two had to carry on alone until April 1588, when Sir Thomas Cecil, who had previously served in Lincolnshire, joined the Northamptonshire deputation. Cecil's frequent absences, however, meant that he was unable to pull his full weight, and in February 1590 Sir George Fermor was appointed as a fourth deputy, "for that there are not in number sufficient to discharge her Majestie's service there".[2]

One of the main tasks of those responsible for the militia, whether acting as muster commissioners or deputy-lieutenants, was to ensure that all men of substance in the shire fulfilled their statutory obligations to possess arms and armour in quantities commensurate with their wealth.[3] This was no easy task; the wealthier inhabitants, who were also obliged to keep horses and all necessary "furniture" for demi-lances and light horsemen, were notoriously neglectful of their obligations. Matters came to a head in November 1580 when the government, deeply concerned about the national shortage of horses and horse-armour, appointed general commissioners for "the musteringe of horsemenn and for the orderinge and breedinge of horses" in every part of the realm (4). The execution of the commission in Northamptonshire and eight other shires was delegated to Sir Christopher Hatton and the Earls of Leicester and Warwick, who in turn handed over responsibility to local commissioners, who were required to report on the situation in their particular shires. The Northamptonshire Commissioners seem to have acted promptly; in response to the lords' enquiry, dated 10 November, they returned their certificate before the month was out. But the report was not very satisfactory. With regard to the breeding of horses they informed the lords that "theire groundes for breed ... are all dulye kept according to the Statute", but failed to certify "the nomber of theire groundes, mares [and] stallondes". With regard to the number of horsemen they reported that the shire could furnish 20 demi-lances and 80 light horsemen, making a total of 100—a suspiciously round-looking

[1] P.R.O. SP 12/162/12. Sir Edward Brudenell, who had been a deputy-lieutenant under Parr, was apparently added to the number in 1584: J. Wake, *The Brudenells of Deene* (2nd edn., 1954), p. 60.
[2] *A.P.C.* xviii. 334. Fermor lived in the western division, which, since Knightley was then in prison, was without a deputy-lieutenant.
[3] For these obligations, see Boynton, pp. 9-11. It should be noted that the clergy were assessed separately by their own officials; *ibid.*, pp. 33ff.

sum.[1] With this assessment the lords were not satisfied and suggested that the local commissioners had under-estimated men's "habilites"; they therefore raised the assessments of some of those on the list and returned the document to the senders, with the request that they should add the names of others in the shire who were "of abylitie to kepe horses" (2). According to the lords' calculations the shire ought to provide a total of 45 demi-lances and 142 light horsemen.[2] Following the receipt of the lords' letters musters were held at Northampton and Kettering in January 1581, where the commissioners, having added 61 names[3] (including those of sons and younger brothers of men already listed and also of some comparatively obscure men, who were each charged with half the cost of equipping a horseman), then endeavoured to enforce the new rate upon the shire. Understandably they met with opposition: Sir Edmund Brudenell objected to his new assessment of two demi-lances and three light horsemen and only sent one horseman to the muster; Edward Andrew, one of the additional 61, pleaded poverty and sent none.[4] Eventually the county reported back to the lords that they were unable to furnish the appointed number, but the privy council were not to be swayed; they expressed sorrow that "of all the sheers of England we should receiue from you only this kind of awnswer", threatened to bring the matter to the personal attention of the Queen, and ordered the commissioners to try again.[5] In spite of all this pressure, however, the Northamptonshire gentry remained obdurate. In August 1583, when the government came to review the situation, it was noted that their shire, unlike some others that had eventually succeeded in meeting their requirements, was still in default.[6] And at the musters taken in the western division in the following month the numbers of horsemen viewed again fell far short of the quota for the division;[7] as a result, when the commissioners came to report their proceedings at the end of September, they were evidently still insistent that 100 was the most that the shire as a whole could furnish.[8]

The subsequent history of the struggle between the privy council and the Northamptonshire gentry is not easy to untangle. What is certain is that in September 1586 the council, in making plans for an army to attend the Queen in the event of invasion, appointed Northamptonshire to provide 200 horsemen[9]—slightly more than the number originally rated on the shire. Accordingly at some date after this Knightley and Montagu, newly appointed as deputy-lieutenants, set about the task of trying to meet the council's demands. What happened in the eastern division is not clear,

[1] P.R.O. SP 12/162/12 (1). This document, dating from 1583, contains an abstract of the certificates made in 1580 and 1581.
[2] The assessed totals are given as 46 demi-lances and 147 light horsemen in *M.B.S.*, p. lxiii; but these figures were derived from a mis-reading of the schedule in P.R.O. SP 12/162/24. That the lords' rate was fixed at 45 demi-lances and 142 light horsemen in 1580 is clear from the entry in Knightley's book (Northants R.O. K2683, p. 20), wrongly dated 1586 in *M.B.S.*, p. 12. The mis-dating of this entry has led to further confusion over events in 1586 and 1587 in *M.B.S.*, p. lxiv and Boynton, pp. 84-85.
[3] The additional names are found in P.R.O. SP 12/162/24. They are marked with an asterisk in 3.
[4] *M.B.S.*, p. lxiii; H.M.C. *Buccleuch*, iii. 21.
[5] See Appendix 1.
[6] P.R.O. SP 12/162/12.
[7] *M.B.S.*, 184-85.
[8] *Ibid.*, p. lxiii.
[9] P.R.O. SP 12/194/7.

but in the western division the leading residents were charged to find a total of 81 horsemen[1]—only two short of the number rated on the division in 1580. Since some of those previously charged were now dead or had left the shire (16), new names had to be added to the list; some of these were the heirs of those who had died, but others were the representatives of families not previously charged. In the latter category came men who had recently joined the ranks of the local gentry, chief among whom was Sir Christopher's nephew, Sir William Hatton; but most of the new names were those of less substantial inhabitants such as one Love of Aynho, who was so obscure that no-one seems to have known his Christian name. However, what is most noticeable about the assessments is that the more prosperous people had succeeded in reducing their commitments; Knightley himself, who had been charged with six horsemen in 1580, was now charged with only four. The new rate in fact was never implemented, because in April 1587 Hatton informed his deputies that, thanks to his persuasion, the council had agreed to reduce the shire's quota (for the time being at all events) to 100 horsemen (42); and so when this number was confirmed on 11 October (46) the deputy-lieutenants were able to reduce their divisions' charges still further. The rate drawn up for the western division on 18 October (48) shows the incidence of the reductions: Thomas Andrew and Richard Chetwode, for example, each had their assessment lowered by one demi-lance; while Knightley and Hatton, together with a number of poorer men, appear to have had their charges waived completely.[2] Even so, when Knightley and Montagu, having completed their view of the 100 horsemen, reported back to their lord lieutenant at the end of October, they could not resist adding a suggestion that Lord Mordaunt and Lord Compton might be asked to help ease the county's burden.[3] Mordaunt and Compton were two of the " honorable and noble personages " resident in the shire who had not been charged by the deputies (17, 18); peers of the realm and privy councillors were exempt from the county assessments because in the event of war they had to provide their own private contingents of men. The deputies' suggestion, therefore, was a revolutionary one, and naturally nothing came of it; but it does indicate that, after seven years of haggling, as the result of which they seem to have established their claim that 100 horsemen was the most that they could furnish, the Northamptonshire gentry were still looking for ways of reducing their quota.[4]

Another cause of conflict between the central government and the localities was the requirement, introduced in the 1570s, that counties should provide regular training for selected " bands " of footmen.[5] Training, which was supposed to take place on ten days in every year, was an expensive business; wages had to be paid to the soldiers and large quantities of ammunition had to be purchased. The shires, who had to bear the full cost, not unnaturally declared themselves to be overburdened

[1] See the " rate " printed in *M.B.S.*, p. 19, where the date is given as 10 Oct. 1587; it is probable, however, that the rate was drawn up in the previous winter—and almost certainly before April 1587, when the county's quota was reduced to 100.

[2] Knightley and Hatton not only have reduced numbers against their names, but their names have been placed on what looks like a " reserve list ".

[3] See Appendix 2.

[4] In 1590 Montagu informed Hatton that the shire could not furnish 100 horsemen because so many chargeable persons had died or left the county; see Appendix 3 and 4.

[5] See Boynton, pp. 91-96.

and tried hard to reduce the numbers of their trained men. In the face of widespread opposition the government appears to have abandoned the attempt to make training universal and to have concentrated its attention on the maritime counties, where the risks of enemy attack were greatest. It was only in 1586, with the growing danger of a Spanish invasion, that a full scheme of training was imposed on all inland shires. Thus one of Hatton's first tasks, after his appointment as lord lieutenant in September of that year, was to pass over to his deputies the council's instructions regarding the selection of 1,000 footmen for the bands (**9**). As was always the case with trained bands, the men had to be very carefully chosen; the bands were, " as neere as may be ", to " consist of such househoulders as for their personage shalbe founde seruisable and of lyving and hauiour able to beare the charge of the traynynge ". In order that the deputy-lieutenants should know precisely what " the forme of theire traynynge " was to be, Hatton sent them copies of the various orders that had been issued to the maritime counties[1] and, in addition, a report of the actual procedure that had been followed in Kent (**5**). The overall direction of training was to be the responsibility of a muster master, who was to be chosen from the ranks of the local gentry and whose duties were fully set out in " Heades of Instructions " (**6**). His principal concern was to be the training of the " shott ": in every band there were to be four " chief trayners " or corporals, who were to instruct the men in the use of their firearms (**11**); understandably, particular stress was laid on the importance of not " endangering them selves and their fellowes " and on the need for economy in the use of powder (**40**).

The government's requirement that 40 per cent of the trained footmen were to be " shott " meant that Northamptonshire, whose quota of footmen had been raised to 1,200 in February 1587 (**38**), had to provide 480 men equipped with firearms. This presented a serious problem, for there was a chronic shortage of suitable firearms in the shire; at the musters taken in November 1586 it had been discovered that for the 2,063 able men in the western division there were only 88 calivers (**24**). In due course Knightley and Montagu informed Hatton of the situation, and the privy council, recognising the inadequacy of the county's " stoare of armour ", agreed to reduce their quota (for the time being at any rate) from 1,200 to 600 (**42**). The council's leniency may reflect an unwillingness to overburden the country at a time of economic hardship;[2] in June 1587, when ordering Northamptonshire to raise 200 men for service in the Netherlands, they relieved the shire of the burden of providing armour for the men, " haveing consideracion of the present dearthe " (**45**). The reduction in the number of footmen from 1,200 to 600, moreover, also eased the county's burden in another way; the number of " pryncipall gentlemen of the Country " required to serve as captains was halved.[3] From the original list of twelve captains of foot (**19**, **21**) six, chosen by the lord lieutenant himself, were appointed (**43**). But the gentlemen selected

---

[1] Perhaps as the result of an oversight, the instructions regarding training appear to have been sent out *twice*—once in October 1586 (see **9**) and again in February 1587 (see **37**, **38**). This helps to explain the existence of duplicate sets of instructions in the present collection.

[2] See above, p. xvi.

[3] The number of captains of horse remained the same even though the number of horsemen had also been halved.

do not seem to have been over-enthusiastic; Montagu's son and heir Edward appears to have declined the responsibility, for Francis Nicolls was quickly appointed in his place; Chetwode, taking advantage of the "dual citizenship" which the possession of lands in more than one county conferred on him,[1] apparently excused himself on the grounds that he was resident in Buckinghamshire. In October, six months after the final choice of captains had been made, only two of the men—Burnaby and Knollys—were reported to be ready and willing to serve. Knightley and Montagu were still waiting to hear from Browne, Pickering and Nicolls, who were all away in London.[2]

By the autumn of 1587, therefore, when definite information reached Northamptonshire about the great preparations being made in Spain for the despatch of a mighty armada against England, Knightley and Montagu could not have felt very confident about the military situation in the shire. It is true that some progress had been made: 600 selected footmen, half of them "shott" and the other half pikemen, had been equipped with armour and weapons;[3] orders had been given for the erection and maintenance of beacons (13, 14, 15);[4] and the chief towns had been charged with the provision of stores of powder (20, 22). But much still remained to be done: the gentry had not yet furnished their appointed numbers of horsemen;[5] the captains had not yet taken command of their bands; and the men had yet to be trained. If the Spanish were to invade these islands the men of the Northamptonshire militia, for all their native strength and courage, would hardly be a match for the best-trained and best-equipped army in Europe. Clearly the two deputy-lieutenants would have a busy winter ahead of them.

The Armada Crisis and its Aftermath

Throughout the winter of 1587-88 Elizabeth and her chief advisers still retained some lingering hopes that peace might be made with Spain and the preparation of the armada abandoned, but by early spring these hopes had evaporated; it therefore became a matter of urgency for the government to have exact knowledge of the military strength of the kingdom. The shires had in fact been requested to provide information about the numbers of their able-bodied men and the nature of their equipment in letters sent out in the previous October (47), but many, including Northamptonshire, had failed to do so.[6] Accordingly on 2 April 1588 a sharp reminder was sent to Hatton (53), who passed it on immediately to his deputies (52). At the same time he gave them a piece of information which they were, for the time being, to keep to themselves; this was that 400 out of the 600 footmen rated upon the shire were intended for an army of 4,000 to be assembled in London. The deputies, who were perhaps playing for time, replied that they were unable to carry out his instructions because they had not received the "warrant of deputacion" which, they insisted, the

[1] See below, p. xxxii.
[2] See Appendix 2.
[3] *Ibid.*
[4] For the beacons see *M.B.S.*, p. lxxxviii.
[5] See Appendix 2.
[6] Boynton, pp. 173-74.

renewal of his commission necessitated;[1] Hatton promptly remedied the situation and urged them to proceed with all possible speed (**55**). Two months later, however, Walsingham had to remind Sir Christopher (**59**) that neither of the shires for which he was responsible—Northamptonshire and Middlesex—had yet returned their certificates nor sent in the lists of "martiall men" which had also been requested in April (**54**). Hatton passed on Walsingham's letters to the deputies and once again urged them to attend to the matter "presently", i.e. immediately (**58**). Nevertheless it was not until mid-July that they eventually sent in the required certificate,[2] which stated that the number of able men in Northamptonshire was 1,240, including 600 trained men under the leading of four captains— Knollys, Burnaby, Nicolls and Browne.[3]

Meanwhile news having reached England that "the Kinge of Spaynes Navye is already abroade on the seas" (**57**), arrangements were being made for three armies to be got together in the south: one to remain in the maritime counties to defend the coasts; another, based on Tilbury, to defend the Thames estuary; and a third to be assembled in and around London to protect the Queen's person. It was to this third army that the forces of Northamptonshire were to be sent.[4] Accordingly on 15 June Hatton wrote from Greenwich to order his deputies to be prepared to send 400 of the 600 trained footmen "to attende here at the Cowrte"; the "conduccion" of the men was to be committed to Knightley, "a gentleman very meete to be employed in the accion of that service" (**56**). During the next four weeks there was an uneasy lull, as the armada lay at Corunna recovering from the ravages of the Biscayan storms.[5] But from 19 July, the day on which, according to legend, Captain Fleming interrupted Drake's game of bowls to report the sighting of the Spanish fleet off the Scilly Isles, there was a great flurry of activity. On that fateful Friday Hatton, who could not yet have heard the news from Plymouth, sent three letters down to Northamptonshire. Two were to his deputies: one ordered them to make ready not only the 400 trained men already standing by but also "the whole forces of that Countie both of horse and footmen", who were to be prepared to march to London within a week (**62**); the other required them to levy coat and conduct money for the soldiers from the inhabitants of the shire (**61**).[6] The third letter, addressed to Knightley alone, reminded him that he was to conduct the men to London and warned him yet again that the Northamptonshire contingent must not be inferior to that sent by any other shire (**63**). Four days later Hatton informed Knightley that, since the armada was now sailing along the English coast and an invasion by the Duke of Parma seemed imminent, he must with all convenient speed dispatch the 100 horsemen to London; in addition the full number of 600 footmen were to be led to London

---

[1] The new commission, no copy of which appears to survive, and which, according to Hatton, contained "no alteracion in substaunce", was probably necessitated by the addition of Sir Thomas Cecil to the deputation.

[2] See the postscript to Hatton's letter of 19 July (**62**).

[3] *The History of the Spanish Armada* (1759), p. 20.

[4] The original plan was that the men of Northamptonshire and Middlesex should be placed under the command of Sir William Hatton, one of the "coronells"; *ibid.*, p. 27.

[5] For the chronology of the armada's progress, see G. Mattingly, *The Defeat of the Spanish Armada* (1959), where the dates are given according to the "New Style" not adopted in England until the eighteenth century.

[6] For the money collected in the western division, see **72**.

by the 29th (**65, 66**). So desperate was the government becoming that on Sunday, 28 July, when the Spanish fleet lay at anchor off Calais, orders were given for contingents of archers to be raised in every shire; Hatton asked Knightley to see if he could find 200 men in Northamptonshire who were skilled in that ancient but still highly regarded art (**66**).

Down in Northamptonshire preparations were proceeding apace. At some stage Knightley had been able to organise five days' training for the bands of the western division at Towcester and Daventry (**72**), while in the east Montagu had arranged similar sessions at Wellingborough and Oundle.[1] Arrangements had also been made in both divisions for the requisition of carts and carters for the carriage of the arms. By 29 July, the day appointed for the march to London,[2] the men of Northamptonshire were ready. On the 30th Montagu was at Northampton, where he paid the "chardges and allowances" of his two captains, Browne and Nicolls, and wrote a hurried note on the back of the account sheet wishing Knightley "a prospeorovs jorney" (**68**). Apparently the two companies from the eastern division—one of 145 men (including 47 from the soke of Peterborough) under Browne (**70**), and one of 139 men under Nicolls (**71**)[3]—left Northampton next morning and marched to Towcester, where they linked up with the two companies from the western division under Knollys and Burnaby;[4] from there the united county contingent marched to London under Knightley's command.[5] Although they seem to have stopped on the way to practise shooting (**72**), they made exceptionally good progress. With their morale raised by the beating of drums and the distribution of extra money "to have them the more willinge to make the more hast",[6] they probably succeeded in their aim of reaching Dunstable on the first night and London on the second. At any rate from 2 August onwards they were on the pay-roll of Lord Hunsdon's army, assembled on the outskirts of London for the defence of the Queen's person.[7] By that date, however, the real danger was over; the armada had been broken up and its battered ships had turned for home. Even so the government was taking no chances. The army was not disbanded until 14 August, on which day Hunsdon informed the Northamptonshire deputy-lieutenants that, although he was sending the men home, their armour and uniforms should be carefully preserved in some convenient place in case another emergency arose (**74**). He also

---

[1] *M.B.S.*, pp. 193-4. The Bishop of Peterborough and the local J.P.s had arranged the training of the men levied in the soke.

[2] Presumably the order for the men "to be led ... to Londone by the xxixth of this mounthe" (**65**) was taken to mean that 29 July was the latest date for departure.

[3] Since these numbers fall short of the 150 for which the captains had drawn conduct money, Morris suggested that both companies included "dead pays", but the discrepancy can be explained by the presence in each company of others besides the "soldyers". When, two weeks later, Browne marched his company back to Northamptonshire he received conduct money for himself, his lieutenant, two sergeants, two drummers, two clerks and 143 "soldiors". By this date Browne had evidently handed over two of his men to Nicolls to even up the numbers. *M.B.S.*, pp. xxxvi, xcvii-c, and 196. For "dead pays", see Cruickshank, pp. 153-58.

[4] Both men drew conduct money for 150 men (**72**). Knollys in fact had 144 soldiers and Burnaby 143; *M.B.S.*, p. 196.

[5] For an account of the march to London, see *ibid.*, pp. xcviiiff.

[6] The extra payment was apparently made only to the men of the eastern division, who had further to march; *ibid.*, p. 193.

[7] *Ibid.*, pp. 195-96.

asked Knightley and Montagu[1] to deal with four inhabitants of the shire who had refused to serve under Knollys (**73**). Meanwhile the Northamptonshire horsemen under William Lane, who had taken over the command from Hatton's cousin Edward Saunders (**55**), were still on the roll of Leicester's army based on Tilbury, where they had been since 1 August.[2] They remained there until 19 August, when they too were allowed to return to their homes. Significantly, Lane's troop was under strength; apart from himself, his lieutenant, his cornet, a trumpeter, a smith and a clerk, there were only 92 horsemen. The Northamptonshire gentry were evidently sticking to their point that the provision of even 100 horsemen was beyond their poor ability.

After the danger of invasion was past Knightley and Montagu were able to enjoy a more restful time, untroubled by missives from London. Hatton wrote to them on 29 August (**75**), enclosing a long letter from the privy council commending the " care and diligence and travayle " of his deputies and ordering them to enquire into reports of bribery and corruption among the captains of the county levies (**76**). Apart from this —and it is to be hoped that none of the Northamptonshire captains were involved—the deputy-lieutenants appear to have received no further instructions until the following January, when Hatton wrote to them about the loan which the Queen, overburdened by the costs of the war with Spain, proposed to raise from her subjects (**79**). The deputies were not required, as were those in some other shires, to certify the names of those best able to contribute; their task was simply to collect the money that had been demanded in letters sent under the privy seal to individual inhabitants of the shire. " Simply " is hardly the right word, because the collection proved to be an extremely difficult operation. In February Montagu, left to bear the burden alone[3] while Knightley was attending Parliament at Westminster,[4] complained that he had never been " more trubled with any seruice in this County "; he was being inundated with petitions from people asking to be relieved of the burden of paying the loan (**80**). With his letter of complaint he sent Knightley two lists of names for Hatton's attention: one was of people who had received privy seals but who, in his judgment, ought to have their amounts reduced or waived either because their means were insufficient or because they had been charged in other counties (**81**); the other, of 40 additional persons who had not been charged but were well able to pay.[5] Shortly afterwards he sent some further amendments and said that he was still being troubled by petitioners who mistakenly believed that the deputy-lieutenants had been responsible for the original allocation of privy seals and were therefore in a position to cancel them (**82**). Poor Montagu, it seems, was operating very much in the dark; he evidently wrote to Hatton to point out that, without a full list of the names of the recipients of privy seals

---

[1] Sir Thomas Cecil was out of the county at this time, serving as a colonel in Hunsdon's army.

[2] *M.B.S.*, p. 195.

[3] Montagu was also serving as sheriff at this time. Cecil does not seem to have re-appeared on the Northamptonshire scene until 1590.

[4] Through Hatton's influence Knightley was chosen as one of the knights of the shire for this Parliament (**77**, **78**), which was originally summoned for 12 Nov. 1588, but was prorogued until 4 Feb. 1589.

[5] This list is not extant.

and of the amounts charged, he would be unable to proceed further with the business (**83**).

A month later Hatton, much pre-occupied with parliamentary affairs, eventually got round to dealing with the matter of the loans; he informed the deputies that the privy council had agreed to reduce Northamptonshire's total charge from £5,000 to £3,500 and ordered them to use their discretions in reducing the burdens of the individual inhabitants of the shire (**84**). After the final meeting of Parliament on 29 March, at which Hatton made his last and probably most notable speech,[1] Knightley was free to return to Northamptonshire and get on with the task of amending the charges of those in his division. As a result nineteen men, many of whose names had been on Montagu's schedule, had their charges waived completely; six had their amounts reduced; while others who had died or left the shire had their names struck off the list (**85**). On the other hand sixteen privy seals remained unchanged; the recipients had to pay the sums originally demanded (**86**). Among those fortunate enough to have their privy seals cancelled were two residents in the shire who by no stretch of the imagination could have been described as " not hable " to pay the sums demanded : Sir Richard Knightley and his son Valentine (**87**). They— and Montagu in the eastern division—were granted exemption from payment of the loan in view of the expenses that they had incurred in the course of their duties, their claim being that this was a " favour which other Deputy Leaftenantes haue in other Counties " (**81**). In fact, however, such exemptions were not universal; in Sussex, for example, two of the deputy-lieutenants, Sir Thomas Shirley and Walter Covert, each contributed the maximum of £100.[2] If the chief collectors of the loan in Northamptonshire took such an unpatriotic attitude to the Queen's appeal for assistance, it is not surprising that so many lesser folk were equally unresponsive.

As a result of all their adding and subtracting Knightley and Montagu were eventually able to send Hatton a revised schedule of names and sums, but the total still fell short of the required amount by £500. They expressed the hope that the privy council might be content with the sum of £3,000 and in the end, after some special pleading on Hatton's part, they got their way (**88**). But even then they had great difficulty in actually collecting the outstanding money. On 21 May Montagu ordered all those who had not yet made their contributions to do so before 1 June,[3] but by 16 June many had failed to do so. Most of the defaulters were in the western division and he asked Knightley to deal with them promptly (**90**). Knightley's efforts, if he made any, were of no avail; of the 31 defaulters in his part of the county (**91**) only nine in the end paid up.[4] The final total levied throughout the whole shire was only £2,025, but Northamptonshire was not the only county that failed to reach its target; throughout England the opposition to the loan was widespread and many counties complained that the burden laid upon them was too heavy to

---

[1] Neale, *op. cit.*, p. 237.

[2] T. C. Noble, *The names of those persons who subscribed towards the defence of this country at the time of the Spanish Armada* (Huntingdon, 1886), p. 64 ; H.M.C. 15th Rep. App. V, p. 25.

[3] 30 Northamptonshire men had in fact paid up by the beginning of May. The full list of contributors from the shire is printed in Noble, *op. cit.*, pp. 47-48.

[4] Two of the 31 should not have been listed because they had already been discharged.

be borne.[1] Montagu's complaint that "the generall losse that hath beene this yere in our cuntry ... hath impoverished the cuntry" (**83**) was echoed in Leicestershire;[2] indeed such losses were probably universal. But the real reason for the failure of the shires to produce the money demanded from them was not the poverty of their inhabitants but the traditional unwillingness of Englishmen—and especially the gentry—to contribute to the costs of government. Among those in Northamptonshire who defaulted in 1589 was Sir George Fermor, one of the wealthiest men in the county, who was to be pricked as sheriff later that year and was to be appointed a deputy-lieutenant early in 1590. That a man like Fermor, one of the key men upon whom the central government depended for the implementation of its orders in the localities, could thus flout its authority shows up one of the inherent weaknesses of the Tudor regime. It was in an attempt to remedy such weaknesses that lord lieutenants had been appointed to oversee the administration of the shires, but in spite of all their endeavours the weaknesses remained.

Assessment: Hatton as Lord Lieutenant

When in 1585 Elizabeth revived the commissions of lieutenancy after a lapse of fifteen years some of those who received them were probably in some doubt as to what the work involved. Certainly Hatton, on his appointment as lord lieutenant of Northamptonshire in the following year, could not benefit directly from the experience of his predecessor in the office; William Parr, Marquess of Northampton, who had held the post more or less continuously from 1551 to 1570, had died in 1571.[3] And although general instructions had been drawn up for the new lieutenants, these needed to be interpreted in the light of the particular circumstances of the individual shires. The task was no easy one. The lieutenant in fact had a dual role: he was the representative of the court in the country and the representative of the country at court.[4]

Hatton at the time of his appointment appeared to be well placed to represent the court. He enjoyed the special favour of the Queen. He had been a gentleman of her privy chamber and captain of her guard since 1572, and vice-chamberlain of her household since 1577. From 1577 onwards he was a member of the privy council and a regular attender at its meetings. In common with many privy councillors he therefore participated in the making of the decisions which, as lord lieutenant, he was later called upon to implement in his shire.[5] It often happened that Hatton helped to decide the contents of orders that were later sent to him for execution; normally, and understandably, he did not himself sign such letters, but occasionally he did (**47, 51, 65, 76, 95**). As has been seen, because he was so deeply involved in the business of government he did not personally see to the execution of these instructions, but, like other

[1] Scott Thomson, pp. 123-24.
[2] *A.P.C.*, xvii, p. 317.
[3] Parr had originally been appointed for Bedfordshire, Buckinghamshire, Hertfordshire and Cambridgeshire as well as Northamptonshire.
[4] Cf. Scott Thomson, p. 77.
[5] In 1587 eight of the sixteen active and eligible members of the privy council were also lord lieutenants; Cruickshank, p. 20.

privy councillors similarly commissioned, passed them on to his deputy-lieutenants who were empowered to act " as yf my self were present in persone " (8).

In order that his deputy-lieutenants should fully understand the government's intentions Hatton followed what seems to have been the standard practice of enclosing the privy council's letters in short covering notes of his own.[1] On one occasion he apparently forgot to write a covering letter: in January 1588 a messenger arrived at Montagu's house at Barnwell bearing a letter from the council to Hatton and "saing he hadd noe other letter from my Lord Chauncellor " (51); and the deputy-lieutenants, lacking a "particular order" from Hatton, very properly (or very obstinately) waited for further orders before taking any action (50). Sometimes delays were also caused by Hatton's failure to write promptly to his deputies. His first commission, dated 12 September 1586 (1), was not sent to them until 8 October, possibly because he had delayed action until he had an opportunity to go down to Holdenby. Valuable time was also lost in the following year; the important privy council letter of 20 February (38) was not sent on to the deputy-lieutenants until 15 March (37). In all fairness, however, it should be pointed out that when the situation became critical in the summer of 1588 Hatton was sending on the council's letters on the day they were written (56, 57). The most serious delays that year were not caused by him but by his deputies who, as has been seen, waited until mid-July to send in the certificates demanded at the beginning of April; he had to point out to them that the certificate " hathe ben looked for long since and thowghte sumwhat straunge it hathe not ben hitherto received " (58). But it is also " sumwhat straunge " that he had apparently not written before to remind them about their negligence; in his letter of 15 June (56) he made no mention of the matter, and it was not until Walsingham jogged his memory a few days later (59) that he sent off a reminder to his deputies. It may be that he was having difficulty in keeping up with the demands of his numerous offices; since he was also a privy councillor, lord chancellor,[2] vice-admiral of the Isle of Purbeck and chief commissioner for musters in Middlesex,[3] it was inevitable that he could only give a small part of his attention to the affairs of Northamptonshire.

Hatton's constant pre-occupation with affairs of state and his frequent bouts of illness, which sometimes delayed his correspondence (78), were not the only things that were likely to prevent him being an effective lord lieutenant. A major disqualification for the office was his total lack of military experience: he had not served in Ireland or the Netherlands; he had never acted as a local commissioner of musters and therefore had no first-hand knowledge of selecting, training and equipping men for war; nor did his captaincy of the Queen's guard constitute a qualification, since the guard's duties were mainly decorative. He was therefore in no position

[1] Hatton normally sent the original privy council letters; only rarely (9, 45, 95) did he send copies.
[2] From 29 April 1587, when he ceased to be vice-chamberlain and captain of the guard.
[3] The commission was issued in April 1588, but it is clear that Hatton's role was merely supervisory; he was lord lieutenant in all but name. He was formally appointed lord lieutenant of Middlesex on 27 Oct. 1590. See A.P.C., xvi, pp. 33-34 and J. C. Sainty, Lieutenants of Counties, 1585-1642 (1970), p. 27.

to offer the kind of advice that Lord Burghley, no soldier himself but a man with a long familiarity with militia matters, was able to give to his deputy-lieutenants in Essex, Hertfordshire and Lincolnshire; the sets of instructions that the Lord Treasurer sent out in 1587 and 1590, it has been suggested, "reveal careful and intelligent discussion of the problems involved and, in the case of the latter one, some profit from the experience of 1588 ".[1] Even if Hatton had had enough enthusiasm to send such instructions to his deputy-lieutenants it is doubtful if they would have been well received either by Knightley and Montagu, with so many years' service behind them, or by Cecil and Fermor, with their first-hand experience of war in the Low Countries.[2] Again he was in no position to dictate to men whose knowledge of the land and people of Northamptonshire was so much greater than his own. Although born and bred in the shire, he had spent very little time there since his admission to the Inner Temple in 1560; unlike Burghley, who, when lord lieutenant of Essex and Hertfordshire, was often at Theobalds (conveniently situated near the border of the two shires), Hatton rarely visited his country houses. And although he had numerous friends, relations and clients among the Northamptonshire gentry, and had been on the commission of the peace there since 1569,[3] he was probably not very familiar with the social situation of the shire. He more or less admitted as much in April 1587; when it came to the question of choosing gentlemen as captains he conceded that Knightley and Montagu were "better acquainted then my selfe with the state of the Shiere " and particularly with "the disposicion of the gentlemen " (42). Had he been equally ready to acknowledge his ignorance two years later when privy seals had to be sent out for the loan and appropriate people chosen to receive them, fewer demands might have been directed to men who were dead, departed or diminished in estate. "If you and I with the Justices had made certificatt as they did in other Counties ", wrote Montagu to Knightley, "halfe this trubble would haue beene saved " (82). This, of course, is the stock complaint of the local men in the know against the ignorance and ineptitude of distant superiors, but Hatton's deputies did not often have to speak in this vein because he so rarely took decisions out of their hands. On only one occasion is he known to have deliberately over-ruled a local decision; this was early in 1590 when he ordered Montagu to keep the eastern division's powder and match in the central store in Northampton where the rest of the county kept its supply—an arrangement that was highly inconvenient for Montagu who took steps, soon after Hatton's death, to have his decision reversed.[4]

Hatton's unfamiliarity with local circumstances, which inhibited his effectiveness as the court's representative in the country, also placed him at a disadvantage when it came to representing the country at court. To a greater degree than Burghley and some other lord lieutenants he was obliged to rely for essential information upon his deputies, who, like

[1] Conyers Read, *Lord Burghley and Queen Elizabeth* (1960), p. 414. Burghley's instructions are printed in J. Bruce, *Report on the arrangements which were made for the internal defence of these kingdoms when Spain projected the invasion and conquest of England* (1798), Apps. vi and lxv.

[2] Knightley and Montagu had both been depaty-lieutenants under Parr. Cecil was governor of Brill in 1585. Fermor raised 300 volunteers in Northamptonshire and Huntingdonshire for service in the Netherlands in 1586; *A.P.C.*, xiv, pp. 65-66.

[3] It is doubtful if he actually participated in the work of the commission.

[4] *A.P.C.*, xix, pp. 71-72; xxii, pp. 522-23.

deputy-lieutenants everywhere, were ever anxious to convey the impression that their "country" was the poorest and weakest in the realm. Hatton, who was not altogether lacking in local patriotism, was often prepared to collude with them. As has been seen, he was willing to intercede with the privy council to have the county's burdens eased in the matter of the trained bands in 1587 and in that of the loan money in 1589. He was even prepared to put his tongue in his cheek and request that Northamptonshire, which, as Montagu had been at pains to point out, was indisputably smaller and poorer than Lincolnshire (**83**), should have special treatment on the grounds of its "smalleness" or its "povertie"— although he was evidently unsure as to which of these attributes would sound more credible (**88**). But although he was prepared to sympathise with the grievances (real or imaginary) of his fellow-countrymen, there were limits to the lengths he would go in putting their interests before those of the nation as a whole. When, at the height of the armada crisis, the deputy-lieutenants asked him for some "easinge of the charge of the Countye", he was in no mood to pander to their parsimony; he urged them to "consyder the wayght and necessetye of this service" and to be mindful of "the common daunger of the Realme" (**64**). In the end the frequent pleas of poverty proceeding from a shire renowned for its prosperity drove him to the point of exasperation. In July 1591, when men were levied in Northamptonshire for service in France under the Earl of Essex, and the deputy-lieutenants requested reimbursement of the soldiers' coat and conduct money, he rebuked them in the sharpest possible terms:[1]

> We can not but lett you understand how sparinglie and neerelie you have delt in that behalf, and how your dealing dothe differr from that of other counties where like numbers of men have bene leavied ... Theirfore as we doe use to geve thankes to those shires where we finde good forwardnes and inclinacion in those publique services, soe we cannot but lett you playnly understand of the want we have juste cause to note of your doinges above all other counties of the realme, whereof as generally we have all of us occasion to myslike of your nere dealling herein, so I, the Lord Chaunccllor, beinge her Majesty's Lieutenante of that countie, have just cause to finde my self verie much agreaved.

The lord lieutenant's role as the connecting link between the privy council and the shire was clearly a most difficult one to sustain—and for Hatton particularly so. He was under enormous pressure from both sides. On the one hand, being a courtier who owed everything to the Queen's favour, he had to maintain his credit as a faithful and efficient servant of the Crown; hence his constant reminders to his deputies that their reputations and his were at stake (**37, 44, 58**, etc.). On the other hand, being something of a *homo novus* in Northamptonshire, he had to have a care for his reputation in the county; hence his anxiety to give the impression that, thanks to his great influence at court, Northamptonshire enjoyed a specially privileged position among the shires. But was this really so? In June 1588 he spoke of "the greate favour vowchesafed vnto vs by her Majestie" in charging the shire with the provision of a mere

[1] *Ibid.*, xxi, pp. 308-9.

400 men, "where everie other Shiere of the Realme is to supplie allmoste thrice the dubble of that number" (**56**); in other words he was suggesting that every other county in England was being charged with at least 2,000 men. However, an examination of the original lists of "numbers of men appointed to bee drawen together to make an army for the defence of her Majesties person" (which probably dates from early June 1588) reveals that he was guilty of gross exaggeration. Only four shires—Essex, Kent, Norfolk and Suffolk—were charged with as many as 2,000; and at the other end of the scale Leicestershire and Huntingdonshire were charged with 500 and 400 respectively.[1] Nevertheless the reduction of the Northamptonshire quota, albeit only temporarily,[2] to that allocated to the much smaller county of Huntingdon shows that Hatton did have some success in easing the burden of his native shire. At the same time, however, he was also looking after the interests of Middlesex, where he had his principal residence (Ely Place) and where he was lord lieutenant in all but name;[3] in the previous April he had persuaded the council to reduce that shire's number from 1,500 to 1,000.[4] It would be interesting to know if, when writing to the gentry of that county, he informed them, as he informed his deputies in Northamptonshire, that "noe other Shire of the Realme be nighe soe well and favorablye delt with all as ours, I cann assure you" (**64**).

All things considered Hatton was probably no more or no less effective as a lord lieutenant than anyone else in a similar position. It is true that those lieutenants who were not also privy councillors, such as Lord St. John in Huntingdonshire,[5] had more time to give to the work and were often able to maintain closer links with their shires. But those who were caught up in affairs of state were invariably obliged to leave most of the work to their deputy-lieutenants. Even Burghley, for all his zeal and energy, had to do so. It is indeed interesting to speculate how things might have turned out if Burghley, who appears to have coveted the post,[6] had been appointed lord lieutenant of Northamptonshire in Hatton's stead. He might have given closer and more expert supervision to the levying and training of the bands[7]; he would probably have had greater success in raising the loan;[8] he might, with the help of his son Thomas, have exercised greater personal influence in the shire—and especially in the north-east of it where he enjoyed considerable authority as the lord of the liberty of Nassaburgh (**42**). But it is doubtful whether even he would have had much success in breaking down the local particularism of the Northamptonshire gentry and in overcoming their extreme reluctance to fulfil their military and financial obligations to the Crown. Northamptonshire

---

[1] P.R.O. SP 12/211/73. In this list, it should be pointed out, Northamptonshire was charged with 1,000 men; perhaps Hatton later persuaded the council to reduce the number to 600. In the cases of Leicestershire and Huntingdonshire, however, the numbers on the list correspond to those subsequently demanded; see *A.P.C.*, xvi, p. 171 and W. M. Noble, *Huntingdonshire and the Spanish Armada* (1896), pp. 16-17.

[2] In July he failed to persuade the council not to raise the number from 400 to 600; see **60, 65**.

[3] See above, p. xxviii.

[4] *A.P.C.*, xvi, pp. 33-35.

[5] See W. M. Noble, *op. cit., passim.*

[6] Conyers Read, *op. cit.*, p. 413.

[7] See above, p. xxix.

[8] His careful supervision of the collection of the loan in Essex seems to have produced good results; see Scott Thomson, p. 123 and Conyers Read, *op. cit.*, p. 581, n. 11.

in any case was an exceptionally difficult county to govern. Its extent was considerable; even Hatton, who may never have traversed the length and breadth of it, realised that it was hardly accurate to speak of its " smallenes " (**88**). Its geographical position, wedged in between so many other shires, made it inevitable that a proportion of the gentry (and a higher one than in most shires) would have property in other counties; this could mean that, when threatened by privy seals or assessments for horse-armour, they could sometimes manage to " haue lefte the Cuntrie " before the threat materialised.[1] In 1589, when the loan was being raised, some of them may have been in the position of a certain gentleman who, owning land in Huntingdonshire and Cambridgeshire, was " hoping to have fallen to the ground betweene two stools and so to have bene in both shiers forgotten ".[2] But it was perhaps easier for a gentleman to be " forgotten " in Northamptonshire than in any other shire in the realm; new families were coming into the county in such numbers[3] that it must have been very difficult to keep track of them. Hatton could be forgiven for not knowing much about " the disposicion of the gentlemen " when there were so many comings and goings among them.

When Hatton died, on 20 November 1591, prematurely worn out by the burdens he had borne, no successor was appointed as lord lieutenant of Northamptonshire. This was no reflection on him or on the shire; it was in line with the general policy of the Crown. After the Armada crisis had passed, even though the fear of invasion remained, Elizabeth abandoned the policy of appointing lieutenants over every shire in the realm; and when a lieutenant died he was normally not replaced. Perhaps this is an indication that the experiment had not been an unqualified success and that the best course of action was to return the control of the militia to the men who all along had borne the brunt of the lieutenancy's work—the leading families resident in the shires.[4]

Postscript: 1591-1615

For a few years after Hatton's death there was little military activity in Northamptonshire; it was not until 1595, when there were renewed fears of a Spanish attack, that the gentry of the shire were once more forced to think seriously about musters and training. In August of that year the privy council wrote to the sheriff (John Reade), Sir Thomas Cecil, Sir Richard Knightley, Sir Edward Montagu, Sir William Hatton and Sir John Spencer[5] to inform them that, since Northamptonshire lacked a lord lieutenant, they had been appointed commissioners of musters for the shire and were to see to the execution of all former orders.[6] The gentry, who were clearly reluctant to resume their military duties, replied that the resumption of training would cause hardship to the local inhabitants

---

[1] See Appendix 3.

[2] W. M. Noble, *op. cit.*, p. 53. The passage is quoted in full in Boynton, p. 178.

[3] See A. Everitt, " Social mobility in early modern England ", *Past and Present*, no. 33 (1966), pp. 63-64.

[4] Cf. Scott Thomson, pp. 70-73.

[5] The son of the Sir John who had died in 1586. The council later added the names of Sir George Fermor and Robert Wingfield to the list of local commissioners.

[6] H.M.C. *Buccleuch*, iii. 36. For the former orders referred to in the letter see **92**.

IN VITA FORTVNA
LO. HETHERTO, BY HELPE OF HEVENLIE POWERS
MY DOVTFVIL LIFFE HATH RONNE HIS POSTINGE RACE
WHOS RECKLESSE YOV THE HATH PAST SVCH STORMIE SHE
AS MIGHT HAVE CVTE ME OF IN HALFE THIS SPACE.
YET MIGHTIE IOVE BY HIS CELESTIALL GRACE
HATH BROGHT MY BARKE TO SVCH A BLISFVIL SHORE
AS DAYLIE DOTHE ADVANCE ME MORE AND MORE
IN VITA FORTVNA.

A · 1567
ÆTATIS SVÆ · 33

SIR RICHARD KNIGHTLEY

(Reproduced by permission of Viscount Gage, Firle Place, Sussex)

and asked for a moratorium until the next year. At the same time, perhaps in the hope of gaining some respite, they requested letters of deputation similar to those that had been issued in Hatton's day.[1] But the council were not to be put off by such tactics: since there was no lord lieutenant there could be no letters of deputation; and musters could not be postponed beyond October. All excuses having failed the gentry were obliged to get on with their assignment, but the results of their labours did not meet with the privy council's approval; the commissioners were informed that their muster certificates were deficient and their programme of training inadequate.[2] In 1596, when a full-scale Spanish invasion seemed imminent, the council re-issued their instructions and, in addition, ordered the shire to recruit troops for service in Ireland, where the danger of attack was greatest.[3] However, it was not until 1599, when there was an even more serious invasion scare, that there was anything approaching a repetition of the proceedings of 1588; in this year, the last one of the old century, the shire was once again ordered to provide large numbers of horsemen and footmen for the defence of southern England.[4]

After 1599, as the danger of invasion receded, the shires of England became increasingly neglectful of their military responsibilities; regular musters and training were abandoned and, in Northamptonshire as elsewhere, men were able to put away their pikes and calivers and devote their spare time to more peaceful pursuits. In 1605, however, the newly elevated Earl of Exeter (formerly Sir Thomas Cecil and from 1598 second Baron Burghley) made a bold attempt to revive the martial enthusiasm of the shire. Appointed lord lieutenant of Northamptonshire soon after the accession of James I in 1603, he took his responsibilities rather more seriously than some of his colleagues in other counties and, in ordering training in 1605 and musters two years later, he was in fact exceeding his instructions.[5] His deputy-lieutenants—Sir Richard Knightley, Sir Edward Montagu,[6] Sir Anthony Mildmay, Sir Arthur Throckmorton, Sir George Fermor, Sir William Lane and Sir William Tate—did not altogether share his enthusiasm, and very little seems to have been achieved. It was not until 1613, when the old fears of foreign invasion were temporarily revived, that Exeter succeeded in overcoming the reluctance of some of the gentry to re-introduce regular musters and training. In the musters taken that year in the western division Knightley, although now turned eighty, appears to have taken an active part; it was partly due to his initiative and industry that full lists of arms and weapons were drawn up (**97**). When musters were taken again in 1614 Knightley, it seems, took a less active part; at the end of the year his son-in-law Sir Euseby Andrew, who was staying with him at Norton, was evidently helping him with the business of handing over the major responsibility for the western division to his younger colleague Sir William Tate (**96**). In the following September the old knight died, leaving behind him a distinguished record of public service; a deputy-lieutenant under Parr, Hatton and Exeter, he had been

[1] H.M.C. *Buccleuch*, iii. 37.
[2] *Ibid.*, p. 45.
[3] *Ibid.*, pp. 48-49; *M.B.S.*, pp. 32-35; cf. Boynton, pp. 191ff.
[4] H.M.C. 15th Rep. App. v. p. 106.
[5] For the history of the Northamptonshire militia in the years 1605-15, see *M.M.B.*, pp. li-lvii. Cf. Boynton, pp. 210-11, 213-14.
[6] The son of the former deputy-lieutenant, who had died in 1602

actively involved in the administration of the county for over forty-five years. Thanks to his industry and enthusiasm the militia of the western division had been kept equipped and trained for war at a time when England was continually being threatened by invasion. Thanks to his care in preserving so many of the letters and papers relating to this service later generations have been able to piece together something of the history of those eventful years.

1. [*fo.* 6b]   [THE QUEEN'S COMMISSION[1] TO SIR CHRISTOPHER HATTON OF THE LIEUTENANCY OF THE COUNTY OF NORTHAMPTON. 12 September, 1586. (*Copy*)][2]

ELIZABETH by the grace of God Quene of England, Fraunce and Ireland, Defender of the Faithe, etc. To our trustie and righte welbeloued Counsailor, SIR CHRISTOFER HATTON, knighte, our Vicechamberlaine. GREETINGE.

Knowe ye that for the greate and singuler truste and confidence we haue in your approued fidelitie, wisdome and circumspeccion, we haue assigned, made, constituted and ordeyned, and by theis presentes doe assigne, make, constitute and ordeyne you to be our Lieuetenaunte within our Countie of Northampton and all corporate and priuileged places within the limittes [and[d]] [or[i]] precinctes of the same Countie, aswell within liberties as without. And dooe by theis presentes giue full power and aucthorytie vnto you, that you from tyme to tyme maye levie, gather and call together, all and singuler our subiectes of what estate, degree or dignitie they or anye of them be, dwellinge or inhabitinge within our said Countie and within all places corporate and priuileged within the limyttes or precinctes of the same Countie, aswell within liberties as without, mete and apt for the warrs, and them to trye, arraye and put in reddienes, and them also and euerie of them, after their abilities, degrees and faculties, well and sufficientlie to cause to be [arrayed[d]] [armed[i]] and weaponed, and to take the musters of them from tyme to tyme in places most mete for that purpose after your good discretion.

And also the same our subiectes soe arrayed, tryed and armed, aswell men of armes as other horsemen, archers and footemen, of all kyndes and degrees mete and apte for the warres, to conducte and leade aswell againste all and singuler our enemyes, as also againste all and singuler rebelles, traitors and other offenders and their adherentes against vs, our crowne and dignetie, within our said Countie and all places corporate and preuileged within the limittes or precinctes of the same Countie, aswell within liberties as without, from tyme to tyme as often as nede shall requier by your discretion, and with the said ennemies, traytors and rebelles to fighte, and them to [invayde[d]] [inuade[i]], resiste, represse and subdue, sley, kill and put to execution of deathe by all waies and meanes by your said good discretion.

And to dooe, fulfill and execute all and singuler other thinges wich shalbe requisite for the leuiynge and gouernment of our said subiectes, for the conseruation of our person and peace, so by you in forme afforsaid leuyedd and to be ledde. And to doe, execute and vse againste the said enemies, traitors, rebelles and such other lyke offenders and their adherentes as necessitie shall requier by your discretion, the lawe called

---

[1] The erasures and insertions in this document are in a different hand to the text.
[2] This Commission is printed in Scott Thomson, pp. 153-156, and in *M.B.S.*, pp. 1-4.

the Marshall Lawe accordinge to the Lawe Marshall, and of suche offenders apprehended or beinge broughte in subiection to save whome you shall thinke good to be saved, and to sley, distroye and putt to execution of deathe suche and as manie of them as you shall thinke mete by your good discretion to be put to deathe.

And further our will and pleasure is, and by theis presentes we doe giue vnto you full power and aucthoretie that incase anye [envation[d]] [inuasion[i]] of enemies, insurrection, rebellion, ryottes, routes or vnlawfull assemblies, or any lyke offences shall happen to be moved in [any places of[i]] this our Realme out of the lymittes of this our Commission, that then and as often as you shall perceaue anye suche mysdemeanors to arrise, you with all the power you can make shall with all diligence repayre to the place where anie such invation, vnlawfull assemblie or insurrection shall happen to be made, to subdue, represse and reforme the same, aswell by battayle or other kynde of force, as otherwyse by the lawes of our Realme and the Lawe Marshall according to your discretion.

And further we giue you full power and aucthoritie for the execution of this our Commission, to appoynte and assigne in our said Countie and all corporate and priuileged places aforsaid, aswell within liberties as without, mustermasters and one provoste marshall, which provoste marshall shall execute and vse the Marshall Lawe in case of anye invation or rebellion, in conductinge anye nombers of men of warr againste the said invadors, traitors or rebelles, and duringe the contynuance of suche invation or rebellion. Wherefore we will and commaunde you our [sayd[i]] Leivtenaunte that with diligence you doe execute the premisses with effecte.

And for asmuche as it may be that there shalbe iust cause as nowe there is for you to be attendant vpon our person or to be otherwise imployed in our service, wherby this our service of Leivtenauncie comitted to your fideletie can not be by you in person executed in suche sorte as we have appointed the same, therefore we giue vnto you for your better ayde and assistance, and for the better performance and execution of this [same[i]] our service, full power and aucthoretie to appoynte, assigne and constitute by your wryghtinge vnder your hande and seale our trustie and welbeloued Sir John Spencer, knighte, Sir Richard Knightlie, knighte, and Sir Edwarde Mountegue, knighte, to be your Deputies in this said service in our said Countie of Northampton and all corporate and preuileged places within the lymittes or precinctes of the said Countie of Northampton, aswell within liberties as without. And by this our present Comission we giue vnto the said Sir John Spencer, Sir Richard Knightlie and Sir Edward Mountague, soe beinge by you assigned and appoynted as abouesaid, or to anye two of them, full power and aucthoritie in your absence to doe and execute in our said Countie of Northampton and all corporate and priuileged places within the lymittes or precinctes of the same Countie of Northampton, aswell within liberties as without, all and [anye[d]] [every[i]] thinge and thinges before by this our Comission assigned and appoynted by you to be donne and executed.

And our pleasure, will and commaundement is that your said Deputies shall, ymediatelie after your Letters of Deputacion to them made as is aforesaid, take charge and care to see euerye poynte of this our

Comission as fullie and perfectlie executed in your absence as you your selfe oughte to have donne it yf you had bin presente. And the better to inhable them so to doe, our will and pleasure is that, ymediatlie after suche deputation made as afforesaid, you shall deliuer vnto them a true transumpte of this our Comission subscribed with your hande. And whatsoeuer you, or in your absence your said Deputies or anie two of them as abouesaid, shall dooe by vertue of this our Comission and accordinge to the tenor and effecte of the same touchinge the execution of the premisses or anye parte therof, the same shalbe by theis presentes discharged in that behalfe against vs, our heires and successors.

And further we will and commaunde all and singuler our Justices of Peace, mayors, sheriffes, bayliffes, constables, hedboroughes and all other our officers, mynisters and subiectes mete and apte for the warrs within our said Countie of Northampton and in all corporate and priueleged places within the limittes or precinctes of the said Countie of Northampton, aswell within liberties as without, to whome it shall appertaine, that they and euery of them with their power and servantes from tyme to tyme shalbe attendant, aidinge, assistinge, counsailinge, helpinge, and at the commaundement aswell of you as of your said Deputies or anye two of them as abouesaid, in the execution hereof, as they and [anye^d] [every^i] of them tender our pleasure and will aunswere for the contrarie at their vttermost perrilles.

In wytnes wherof we haue caused theis our Lettres of Comission to be sealed with our Greate Seale. Wytnes our selfe at Westminster, the twelfte daye of September in the eight and twentith yere of our Raigne.

Per ipsam Reginam.   Powle.

"CHR: HATTON"

[fo. 9b]   The Transumpt of Her Majesties Commissione graunted to Sir Christopher Hatton, knight, Vicechamberlayne to her Majestie, of the office of Lieutenant of the Countie of Northampton, &c.

2. [fo. 68a] [LETTER.[1] SIR CHRISTOPHER HATTON AND THE EARLS OF WARWICK AND LEICESTER, TO THE COMMISSIONERS FOR THE MUSTERS IN THE COUNTY OF NORTHAMPTON. 30 November, 1580. (Copy)]

After our hartie commendacions. We have receyved from you and others, the Queenes Majesties Commissioners for the Musters in the Countie of Northampton, your certificat of horsemen appointed to be kept within that Countie. And althoughe we therby perceave that you have verye carefullye and diligentlye traveyled therin for the furtherance of her Majesties service, for which you deserve greate thanckes, yet considering in our oppinions that dyvers of those which by you weare rated mighte in respecte of the valewe of their landes be rated to a greater number of horsses, and also that dyvers be not at all rated to kepe anye horsses, who for their habilites mighte have ben rated, we have

---

[1] A summary of this letter is in *M.B.S.*, p. 12, where it is wrongly dated as 1586.

layed downe a new boke of rates, in which we have caused dyvers of those by you before rated, leavinge to you by example therof to put in suche as, being of abylitie to kepe horses, are not yet rated by you, which boke we sende vnto you herewith, as a matter well considered of by vs, hartelye praying you to assemble your selves to geather with asmuche expedicion as you maye, and thervppon what in you lyethe to procure, aswell those thus rated by vs to be content to kepe horses and geldinges according to the effecte of that boke, as also those that shalbe newelye put in by you to do the like, as farre as vppon good consideracion of their abilites you shall thincke to be mete and expedient, havinge respecte therin to the generall service of her Majestie and the Realme, and not to the particuler contentacion of anye private persone, which we doubte not but you will fullye accomplishe according to the speciall trust reposed in you.

And when you shall have fullye proceded therin, we praye you to make thereof a perfecte booke, and the same to sende vnto vs with all thexpedicion you maye. And so we bydd you hartelye fare well. From the Courte, the last of November, 1580.

For those that are alreadye by vs or shalbe by you newlye rated, you maye appointe a further daye of muster, as you shall se convenient.

Your verie lovinge frendes,

AMBROSE WARWICK   ROBERT LEICESTER   CHR: HATTON

[*fo.* 76b)] xx dymilances, iiij^{xx} light horsses.

3. [*fo.* 72a] A RATE FOR THE KEPINGE OF HORSES IN THE COUNTIE OF NORTHAMPTON. [November, 1580.][1]

EST DEVISION	Dimilances	Light horses by the Highe Commissioners appoyntmente
Sir Robert Lane	2	3
Sir Thomas Tresam	3	4
Sir Edmunde Brudenelle	2	3
Sir Edward Mountague	2	4
Edward Griffen, esquire	3	5
John Stafford	1	2
Symon Norwiche	1	2
Edmonde Elmes	1	2
Sir Thomas Cecill	2	2
Sir William Fytzwilliam	2	2
Edward Watson	1	2
*Mawrice Tresam		1
*William Kerckam		1
*Arthure Broke		1
William Saunders	1	2
*John Osborne		1
John Isham	1	1
*John Lane of Walgrave		1

[1] This is in *M.B.S.*, pp. 12-14. For the significance of the asterisks, see above p. xix.

	[Dimilances]	[Light horses]
*William Humfrey of Barton		1
*John Lenton and Humfrey Orme		1
*Thomas Mulsho and John Neale		1
*George Lynne		1
*Thomas Bawde		1
*Thomas Tawide and Robert Catlyn		1
John Pickering		1
Boniface Pickering		1
Fraunces Worseley		1
*Edward Dudley		1
*George Quarles		1
*Fraunces Asheby		1
*James Cleypole		1
*Lady Margaret Zouche		1
*Edward Androwes		1
Henrye Pratte		1
*Lawrence Maydwell		1
*Symon Mallorie and Anthony Muscot		1
John Fosbroke		1
John Norton		1
*Michell Lewes		1
*Gyles Polton		1
*Edward Hasselwod		1
*Owen Raggesdall and Robert Hasselwodd		1
Edward Dallison		1
Edward Barnwell		1
Fraunces Nicolls		1
Edward Hasselrigg		1
Anthonie Jenkinson	1	
*Roger Charnoke		1
Christofer Yelverton		2
Anthonie Morgan		1
Thomas Lawe		1
*John Wingefeld		1
John Mountstevinge		1
Thomas Hacke		1
Mathewe Robinson		1
Andrewe Scarre		1
William Worme		1
Richard Stevenson		1
John Byrd the elder		1
Thomas Wilkenson		1
Somma : -	23	81

WEST DEVISION

Sir John Spencer	3	5
*Thomas Morgan of Heyford	1	
Sir Richard Knightley	2	4

	[Dimilances]	[Light horses]
George Farmar	2	3
Thomas Andrewes	2	3
Isaby Isame	1	1
Roger Cave	2	3
Thomas Lovet	1	2
George Carleton		2
*Vallentine Knightly		1
*Edward Saunders		1
Edward Onley	1	1
*John Worley		1
William Spencer	1	1
*Thomas Knightley		1
*Thomas Wilmar		1
*John Wake		1
Thomas Catesby	1	
*Thomas Furtho		1
Fraunces Saunders	1	1
Richard Burnaby	1	
*John Reade		1
*Randall Goodall		1
*Mistris Shugburghe		1
*Reynolde Braye		1
*William Clarke		1
*Thomas Kerton		1
*Foulke Odell		1
*Samwell Danvers		1
*Crescent Butterye		1
*George Yorke		1
*Thomas Marmyon		1
*Richard Foxe		1
*John Blincko		1
*William Dormer		1
*Jerom Farmar		1
Frances Bernard		2
*Augustyne Crispe		1
William Chauncey	1	1
*Albone Butler		1
*William Pargiter		1
Edward Cope	1	1
John Drydon	1	1
*Thomas Harbye		1
*William Wattes		1
*Fraunces Foxeley		1
*William Hickling		1
*Mistris Tanfeild		1
Summa :-	22	61
Summa totalis :-	45	142

4. [*fo.* 69a] [INSTRUCTIONS FOR THE MUSTERING OF HORSEMEN AND FOR THE ORDERING AND BREEDING OF HORSES. 10 November, 1580. (*Copy*)][1]

NORTHAMPTON

Instruccions geaven the xth of November by Edward, Earle of Lincolne, Lord Admirall of England; Thomas, Earle of Sussex, Lord Chamberlen; Henry, Earle of Huntingdon, Lord President of the Queenes Majestes Counsaile of the Northe Partes; Ambrose, Earle of Warrwick, Master of the Ordinance; Fraunces, Earle of Bedford; Robert, Earle of Leicester, Master of the Horsses; Henry, Lord Hundesdon, Lord Warden of the Marches towardes Scotlande; Sir Henrye Sydney, knight, Lord President of the Counsaile within the Principalitie and Marches of Wales; Sir Christopher Hatton, knight, Vicechamberlen; GENERALL COMMISSIONERS appointed by the Quenes Majestie for the musteringe of horsemenn and for the orderinge and breedinge of horses, etc., in all places within the Realme.

To Lewes Lord Mordant and the reste ther Deputes appointed for the musteringe of horsemenn within the Countye of Northampton.

1. First, you shall as sone as conveniently you maye assemble your selves to consider of euerye parte of the Commission and Instruccions, and thervppon procede to thexecucion therof with asmuche expedicion as reasonablye maye be.

2. Item, for that yt is necessarye that in this time, when all forren Princes beinge neighbors to this Realme be in armes and that the maner of the presente warres do differ from warres in former tymes, all sortes of horsemen sholde be furnished in suche sort as mought be in greatest force bothe offensyve and defensyve, for which purpose onley her Majestie doth desier that the Realme sholde be sufficientlye furnished of all sortes of horsemen, you shall therfore do what in you lyethe to cause all horsemen to be furnished in sorte followinge.

3. Item, you shall geave knowledge to euerye man that is appointed to kepe horses for dymilances, that he have in a readynes for euerye dymilance ether a sufficient stoned horsse or a verye lardge gelding with a strong leather harnes, and ether a steele saddle or a stronge large boulster saddle with all furniture therto belonginge, and for the man a dymilance harnes furnished, a dymilance staffe, a sword and a dagger. And you shall do what you canne to perswade euerye man to have for his dymilance a stoned horsse, and rather a steele saddle then anye other, and euerye parte of the armour and weapon to be good and sufficient.

4. Item, you shall geave knowledge to euerye man that is appointed to keep horsses for a light horseman, that he have in readines for euerye light horse a sufficient geldinge with a stronge saddle and leather harnes, and all other furniture therto belonging, and for the man a corselet furnished, a northen staffe, a case of pystolls, a sword and dagger. And

---

[1] Also in *M.B.S.*, pp. 14-18. This document seems to have been copied rather hurriedly.

you shall do what you cann to perswade euerye man to have the gelding and [every] parte of the armor and weapon to be good and sufficient.

5. Item, you shall geave knowledge to all suche persons as be or shalbe appointed and certifyed to kepe horsses and geldinges to have them with all furniture to the same belonginge, and their armour and weapon presentlie readye to be shewed from tyme to time before vs or before you in our absence, at suche dayes and places as by vs or by you shalbe appointed.

6. Item, you shall geave knowledge to euerye persone that is appointed to kepe horses for dymilances or for light horsemen, that they do the xjth of Januarye make shewe before vs or before you in our absence, in one certen place which you shall appointe as you shall thinck to be moste fytte for the wholl Shier, of their horsses, armour, weapon and all other furniture, with a sufficient man vppon euerye horsse armed and furnished as is before specified, to thende a perfecte vewe maye be taken therof, and her Majestie certified accordinglye.

7. Item, you shall at the daye appointed in our absence, repaire to the place appointed and shall take a perfecte vewe of euerye horse, armour and weapon presented by anye man before you, and shall consider therof, and see whether the same bee sufficient and fytte for service or no. And wheare you shall fynde defectes, you shall geave order to have the same to be presentlye amended, and shall appointe on [sic] other daye and place as short as maye be, for the shewe onley of suche horsses, armour and weapon as ought to be newlye and better supplyed in place of the former vnserviceable.

8. Item, so sone as you shall have taken your first vewe, you shall make a perfecte muster booke of the names of the persones that kepe the horsses, geldinges, armor and weapon, and of the persones that shall ryde vppon the horsses and geldinges and weare the armour and weapons, and therin shall make trewe declaracion of the sufficiency of euerye of them, and of such defectes as you shall appointe to be reformed against the next vewe, which booke signed with all your handes, or the moste parte, you shall sende vppe to vs with all expedicion, to thende we maye consider who have moste readelye and sufficientlye dischardged his dutie in this behalfe, and also make trewe certificat therof to her Majestie, who dothe earnestlye call vppon us for the same.

9. Item, you shall geave order to all suche persons as shall in sort aboue wrytten make shewe to you of ther horses, armour and weapon, that they have the same contynuallye in a readines for the service of her Majestie and defence of the Realme, so as they maye from tyme to tyme make shewe therof as they shalbe appointed, so as alwaye the same maye be kepte in the stable from the firste of November to the first of Maye yerelye.

TOWCHINGE THE BREEDINGE OF HORSSES AND KEPING OF MARES AND STALLANDES

1. Firste, you shall cause a trewe enquirey to be made of euerye parke within the Countye of Northampton kepinge deare, that shall conteyne a myle [about[a]] in compasse or more, and shall so neare as you canne be

trulye enformed of the trewe circuite of euerye thees parkes, beinge either the parkes of the Queenes Majestie or of anye other person.

2. Item, you shall cause a trewe enquirey to be made of euerye seuerall pasture within the said [Contre[i]] connteyning a myle or mo in compasse, and shall, so neare as you canne, be trulye enformed of the trewe circuite of euerye suche pasture.

3. Item, you shall cause a trewe enquirey to be made of euerye common within that Shier, and of all the townes that do enter common vppon euerye common.

4. Item, you shall cause a perfet boke to be made of euerye the said parkes and pastures and of their seuerall cercuites, and who bee the owners of them, and of the said commons and townes that do enter common.

5. Item, you shall take orther that euerye man that hathe a park of his owne, or in lease, or in kepinge for terme of lief, of the compasse of one myle, shall kepe in the same two mares. And euerye man that shall have a parke of the compasse of iiij myles, shall kepe iiij mares accordinge to the scantlinge appointed in the Statute.[1] And you shall do what you canne to procure euerye man that hathe a parke of ij myles and vpwardes to iiij myles, shall kepe iiij mares of that scantlinge which we take to be the meaninge of the Statute.

6. Item, for that the breede of horsses is so necessarye a matter for the generall defence of the Realme, and is also commodyous to suche as shall brede them, if they be well vsed, you shall perswade with all men that have greate pastures to kepe mares in their seuerall pastures accordinge to the seuerall rates before appointed for parkes.

7. Item, you shall take order that no horsses be kepte vppon anye common in anye place within your Shire which shalbe of lesse scantlinge then is conteyned in the Statute, for which purpose you shall geave warninge to all townshippes to remove the same before the last of Marche. And for that [it] is maniefeste that by the lacke of trewe execution of this Statute ther be at this presente verye fewe or no horsses kepte vppon anye common which be of the scantlinge appoynted by the Statute, wherby the brede of horses is greatlie decayed, to the greate weake[n]ing of the Realme, it shall therfore be verye necessarye that you do travayle with the lordes of euerye common, and with the townshippes that do enter common uppon euerye common, that at their common charge or otherwise, as they shall thincke mete, they do provyde presentlye horses in nomber and scantlinge sufficient to be put vppon the common accordinge to the quantitye of the common, so as therby the trewe meaninge of the Statute for the breede of good horses maye take effecte, and the entercommoners lackinge the vse of horses forbydden by the Statute sholde not also lacke sufficient horses for their mares accordinge to the effecte of the Statute, and so by the lacke of bothe a greater inconvenyence sholde ensue in the steade of a convenient reformacion.

8. Item, you shall perswade all suche persones as shall kepe mares in their parkes or pastures to have sufficient stallandes of their owne if they maye or by the helpe of their freindes, to couer yerelye their mares in due tyme, and you shall make a particuler noote of suche as kepe stallandes

---

[1] The relevant statutes were 27 Hen. VIII, c. 6; 32 Hen. VIII, c. 13; and 8 Eliz. c. 8. These prescribed the "scantling" or height of the horses to be kept.

them selves, and of suche as shalbe provyded by their freindes, to thende you maye from tyme to time have certen knowledge howe euerye man shalbe provyded of his stalland.

9. Item, you shall geave warninge to all persones that be to kepe mares or stallandes to have them provyded and readye before thende of Februarye nexte, so as they maye be to be couered this nexte springe, and you shall perswade them to have the mares and stallandes of as faier and lardge a scantlinge as convenientlye they maye.

10. Item, you shall take a perfecte viewe of all mares and stallande[s] appointed to be kepte within your chardge, and shall make a perfect booke of the names of all persones and townshipes that ought to kepe mares or stallandes, and of the parkes, pastures and commons for the which they oughte to kepe them, and therin to noate who do kepe as they oughte to do, and who do make defaulte and wherein, and therof to make particuler certificat to vs before the xxth of June next.

11. Item, you shall take order that no person shall from henceforthe convey anye horsses or geldinges out of the Realme contrarye to the lawes, statutes and orders therin provyded, wherin you shall not do anye thinge that shall be preiudycyall to the authorytie belonginge to the [authorytie belonge^d] Master of her Majesties horse, by virtue of his office.

And to thintente that the Commission graunted by her Majestie to vs sholde in all places be the better executed, her pleasure is that you, etc. sholde take specyall care to see the Commission executed within the Countye of Northampton. And therfore you shall derecte all your certificates of all your doinges to the Erle[s] of Warwicke and Lecester and Sir Xpofer Hatton, from whome you shall from tyme to tyme receave further dyreccion as shalbe convenient and agreable to her Majesties good pleasure.

E. LINCOLN   T. SUSSEX   A. WARWYCKE   R. LEYCESTER
H. HUNSDON   CH. HATTON

5. [*fo.* 10a]   [DIRECTIONS FOR THE MUSTERS IN KENT. 1585.][1]

i. The Commission was published the xxjth of July at Rochester, my selfe[2] beinge presente, anno 1585.

ii. Their was direction gyven to the generall captaynes for the musteringe and the exercisinge of the trayned bande to the nombre of two thousand fyve hundreth, viz: in the lathes of:—

SUTTON AT HONE: Mr. Justinian Campneys, 300; Thomas Willoughbie, 200.

AYLESFORD: Sir Thomas Fane, knighte, 300; Mr. Thomas Fane, 200; Mr. John Leveson, 200.

SCRAY: Sir Richarde Baker, knighte, 300; Mr. John Cobham, 300.

[1] This document is written on fos. 10, 11a, 12 and 13b (fos. 11-13 forming one quire). The matter on fos. 12b and 13a concerns the beacons in Northamptonshire.
[2] Lord Cobham, lord lieutenant of Kent. See J. N. McGurk, " Armada Preparations in Kent ", *Archaeologia Cantiana*, lxxxv (1970), p. 72.

ST. AUGUSTYNS: Mr. Edward Boys, 200; Mr. Henrie Palmer, 200.
SHEPWAY: Sir Thomas Scotte, knighte, 300.
    [Total:] 2,500
Besides the nombre of 2,500 by order frome the Lordes of hir Majesties
moste honorable Pryvie Counsell, I haue encreased with the good likinge
of the Countrey, viz: in
CANTURBERY: Erasmus Fynche, gent., being captayne, 200.
ROCHESTER: John Wynhall, captayne, 100.
SHEPPEY: [blank] 200.
THANET: [blank] 200.

iii. To the thirde. The whole nombre of able men within the Countie of
Kent to be appoynted to seuerall captaynes, to eche captaine but 100, with
suche furniture as the Countrey is able to yelde.

iiii. The nombre of the light horsemen were willed to furnyshe them-
selves accordinge to the instruction sett downe anno 1584, and placed vnder
seuerall captaynes, eche captayne havinge fyftie or more, viz:
SUTTON AT HONE: Mr. Sampson Leonard, esquire, captain, L [for 50].
AYLESFORD: Roger Twisden, esquire, captain, L.
SCRAYE: William Cromer, esquire, captain, L.
ST. AUGUSTYNS: Sir James Hales, knighte, captain, L.
SHEPWAY: Thomas Scote, esquire, captain, L.
THE BAND OF DEMYLANCES, [blank] L.

Eche of theis captaynes are appoynted to haue a lieuetenaunte, a trompett
and a cornett, and euerie ryder clade in a cassocke of blewe cullor after one
facion.

v, vi. Consideracion hath byne hade of all places of discent, but not
throughlye vewed nor certyfied.

vii. Their is distribucion made of all the trayned bandes of footemen
and horsemen, and seuerall places of rendevous appoynted to repaire vnto
with as convenient spede, viz: as yf the attempte [were] to be made vppon
the Ile of Sheppey, then the three trayned bandes of 700 vnder the conduction of Mr. John Cobham, Mr. Thomas Fane or Mr. John Leveson are
appoynted to repaire to that place, whome the resedewe of the generall bandes
within those lymittes are also appoynted to followe vnder the leadinge of
their seuerall captaynes; and for their more convenient and spedie passage
into the Ile, all the boates of Gillingham, Rochester and Milton are
appoynted to transporte them.
    And yf the ennemye shall lande betwene the Ile of Sheppey and Douer,
then the trayned bandes of the nombre of 700 men in the lathes of Shepway
and St. Augustyns, vnder the charges of Sir Thomas Scotte, Mr. Edward
Boys and Mr. Henrie Palmer are appoynted to be in redynes to repaire to
the place assayled with the generall bandes in those lymittes.
    Yf betwen Folkestone and Rye in Sussex, then the trayned bandes vnder
Sir Thomas Scotte and Sir Richard Baker, to the nombre of 600, shall
repaire to the place assayled with the generall bandes lykewisse.
    The residewe of the trayned bandes not lyeinge neere to encounter the

fyrste attempte of the enemye are to remayne in the seuerall places of rendevous vntill direction be gyven for their repaire forward, least whiles all ronne to one parte of the Shire the enemye giue attempte vpon some other.

[The residue of the trayned bandes*d*]

viii. To eche bande of 300 trayned men their is allotted 50 pyoners, and to a bande of 200, 30 pyoners whose names with their dwellinge places are enrolled. Of which pyoners the counstables of the places where the[y] dwell are appoynted to be their leaders, and to take order for the furnishinge of them with spades, sholles, mattockes, axes, bills and skulles.

ix. To euerie 100 of the trayned men two carriages are appoynted and for the generall bandes after the like rate. The names of the owners of the carriages with their dwellinge places is also enrolled, and for the appoyntinge of vittellers, order shalbe taken with the captaynes to appoynte them.

[*In the margin here opposite the above paragraph is written in column:* Daventry, Dodington, Tychemershe, Gretton, Vfforde in Burrowe Soke, Brington.[1]]

x. Their is order taken with the Justices of the Peace through owt the whole Sheire that the nombre of 300 shotte shalbe in a redynes to be sett on ordynarie nagges vpon the fieringe of the beacons, viz: in the lathes of St. Augustyne, lx[60]; Shepway, lx; Scraye, lx; Aylesford, lx; Sutton at Hone, lx.

[Total:] CCC.

xi. Euerie Justice of the Peace of the Quorum hath promised to fynde two petronelles, and euerie other Justice of Peace one petronell vppon ordynarie geldinges, and the riders to be sewted with cassockes of one cullor, but the Justices of the Peace who haue the leadinge either of the horsemen or footemen do require to be released of their charge, seinge that their owne persons are other wisse imployed.

xii. In euerie place beacons be erected and persons dwellinge therbie be assigned to ouersee the watche therof, and at euerie beacon a keavill is appoynted, by which the watchemen may certeynly discover the fieringe of that beacon frome whome they are to receyve their warninge.[2]

xiii. Their is order gyven to the Justices of Peace for the disarminge of papistes and suspected persons.

xiiij. An othe hath byne mynistred bothe to the captaynes and souldiers of the trayned bandes in all places wher the muster master hath taken muster.

xv. A generall order is gyuen to the muster master in his instructions and to the captaynes that none [shall*d*] shoulde be enrolled in the trayned bandes, but only suche as are farmers or owners or ther sonnes.

---

[1] See **13, 14** and **15**.
[2] See H. T. White, "The Beacon System in Kent", *Archaeologia Cantiana*, xlvi (1934), pp. 77-96.

xvi. I haue written to all the townes to make provision of a proporcion of powder and matche to be in store, wherof parte of them haue provided accordingly, viz:[1]

The towne of Hyth, 429 *li.*; the towne of Lydde, 400; the towne of Sandwich, 426; the towne of Romney, 600; the cittie of Canturberie, 554; the towne of Peuisey [Pevensey], 200; the towne of Rye, 200; the towne of Feversham, [*blank*]; the towne of Fordwich, [*blank*]; the towne of Dover, [*blank*]; the towne of Winchelsey, [*blank*]; the towne of Folkeston, [*blank*]; the towne of Hastinges, [*blank*]; the towne of Seaford, [*blank*]; the towne of Tenderton [*for* Tenterden], [*blank*]; the towne of Gravesende, [*blank*]; the towne of Rochester, [*blank*]; the towne of Myddelston, [*blank*]; the towne of Sittingborne, [*blank*]; the towne of Asheford, [*blank*]; the towne of Tonne-bridge, [*blank*].

[*fo.* 13b] An Order to be sett downe to be observed within the Shere of Kente.

6. [*fo.* 47a] HEADES OF INSTRUCTIONS FOR THE MUSTER MASTERS TO BEE SENT INTO THE INLAND COUNTIES. [September, 1586.][2]

Having made a choise of an apt man to supplie the place of mustermaster, he shall enter into a muster booke the names and surnames of the persons of everie band enrolled with their severall weapons.

Hee shall likewise certefie truly vnto her Majesties Lieutenant the aptnes of the persons enrolled, and in what sort they bee furnished with severall weapons, to thend he may giue order for the reformation of the one and the other.

And whereas the charge of the trayning doth chiefely consist in two thinges, the one in the oft assembling of the said bandes, the other in thexpence of powder, for the avoyding of this inconvenience concerning the first point, it is thought meet that the shott of everie band shall bee trained at such time as the Lieutenant shall apoint, and then the rest of the said bands to bee viewed and trayned together with the shott at the direction of the said Lieutenant. For the second point, which is the avoyding of thxpence of powder, yt is thought convenient that the first training bee made with false fyer, and that everie shott shall haue allowance only of three powndes of powder, which will serve sufficiently both to traine them apart and together with the bands.

And to thend the trayning of the shott apart may be the better performed to the ease of the Contrie, everie captaine shall make choise of fower or fyve out of those which shalbee apointed to bee shott in the severall bands, such as hee shall thinck most apt, to bee instructed by the said captaine and mustermaster in such sort as they may be thorowly taught and made sufficient to traine the rest of the shott according to such direction as they shall receave from the mustermaster, who also shall deliver vnto these selected [bands[d]] persons for trayners the forme and maner [and[d]] of trayning in writing, to thend one uniforme [order[i]] may bee generally observed therein.

[1] This list following is written in column. The figures after each town represent pounds.
[2] Also in *M.B.S.*, pp. 5-7. It was probably enclosed with **37**. See **12** for another copy.

The said chief trayners shall carie the tytle of corporals, whereof in everie band consisting of 80 or 100 persons fower corporals shalbee apointed each to haue vnder him 20 or 24 shott.

For the more ease of the Contrie, everie captaine shall apoint his corporall to traine his shott in some such place as may most fittest bee chosen neer to the habitation of the shott allotted vnto him, according to a direction sent here withall to bee observed by the corporals.

It is also thought meet that the mustermaster him self shall take a view of the whole bands at such time as they shall bee mustered together by order of her Majesties Lieutenant, at the least two severall times, which for the ease of the Contrie [may^d] maie verie well bee done in some holidaie in the after noon after Common Prayer, but not on the Sabaoth daie.

At the first time he shall take a view of their persons and weapons, and yf hee find anie defects in the one or the other, he shall admonish and warn them to see the same reformed against the next generall assemblie.

The second time he shall instruct them in such martiall exercise as by him shalbe thought meet, and take an accompt of the severall corporals howe they haue profited the shott committed to theire chardge.

And yf anie of the enrolled men shall happen to decease, or by sicknes or otherwise [be] made vnable to serve, order must bee taken that their places may bee supplied with able men sorted with like weapons, so as the nomber bee alwaies complete and furnished.

And to the end a spetiall choise bee made of fitt and able men, yt is not meant that the service of anie person whatsoever shalbe excuse to anie retayner to bee exempted or spared, yf otherwise he bee thought fitt.

It shall not bee amisse therefore, in so much as these bands are appointed for the gard of her Majesties person, to signifie vnto you that you make choise of such as are householders, resident within the Shire, and of the welthier sort, having able bodies and well affected in relligion, and that the oath of Supremacie maie bee ministred to the captaines and other officers and souldiers vnder them; whome you maie giue to vnderstand that in case they shall withdrawe them selves from this speciall service, there shalbe a noate taken of them to thend they maie bee emploied in foraine service when there shalbee anie occasion to send souldiers out of the Realme.

It is also thought meet (yf her Majesties Lieutenant shall so thinck good) that the corporals apointed over the shott maie haue the chardge and oversight of the peeces committed to them, to bee the better kept and had in a readines.

You shall further consider with the advice of the Lieutenant, yf some of the said shott maie bee sett on horsback and, in steed of calivers, bee furnished with muskets.

[*fo.* 48b] The Heades of Instructions for the Muster Masters [to be^d] sent into the Inland Counties in Sept. 1586.

[*In another hand:*] For Mr. Vicechamberlain.

7. [*fo*. 16a] [LETTER. SIR CHRISTOPHER HATTON TO SIR JOHN SPENCER, SIR RICHARD KNIGHTLEY AND SIR EDWARD MONTAGU. 8 October, 1586.]

After my right hartie commendacions. Where the Quenes Majestie hath byn latlie pleased to appointe me her Lieutenaunte of her Highnes Countie of Northampton by her gratious Letters Pattentes vnder the Great Seale of England, and hath there in authorized me to depute you three for the better execution of her service in that Countie, for as much as of late I haue receauid letters from the Lordes of her Majesties Pryuy Counsell dyrected vnto me for some present service to be done as by the sayd letters appeareth, the trewe coppie whereof I haue sente you herein closed, kepinge in myne owne handes the originall, these ar to requier you, accordinge to the effecte of the same, to proceed with all cartalnes and good expedition, that her Majesties pleasure in that behalf may be duly performed.

Where in for your more redy proceedinge you shall receave by this bearer my Commission [*No. 1*], which you shall cause, in all places that to your discretions shalbe thought meete, to be read and published. And in your proceedinges here in, you shall haue spetiall regarde to such orders sett downe by my Lordes of her Highnes Pryuy Counsell. as here withall I lyke wyse send unto you.

And soe nothinge doubtinge of your dewtifull cares and thaccomplishment of this her Majesties service, I byd you all right hartely fare well. From my house at Holdenby, the viijth of October, 1586.

Your loving frend,

"CHR: HATTON"

Sir Jhon Spencer
Sir Richard Knightley
Sir Edward Mountague

[*fo*. 19b] To the Right Worshipfull my assured good frendes, Sir Jhon Spencer, Sir Richard Knightley and Sir Edward Mountague, knightes.

8. [*fo*. 15a] [HATTON'S LETTERS OF DEPUTATION TO SIR JOHN SPENCER, SIR RICHARD KNIGHTLEY, AND SIR EDWARD MONTAGU. 8 October, 1586.]

[*Enclosed with No. 7*]

To all men to whome these presentes shall come, I, Sir Christopher Hatton, knyght, her Majesties Vice chamberlayne, one of her Highnes Pryuy Counsell and Lieutenant of her Majesties Countie of Northampton, and all corporat and priuileged places within the lymites or precynctes of the same Countie, as well within liberties as without, send greetinge.

Where as the Quenes Majestie, by her gratous Letters Patentes, bearing date the twelfte day of September in the eight and twentithe yeere of her reygne, hath made, constituted and ordayned me, the sayd Sir Christopher Hatton, her Hyghnes Lieutenant within the sayd countie and all other corporate and priuileged places afore sayde, and by the same hath geuen full power and authority vnto me for the better assisting, performance and executione of her Majesties sayd Commissione, to appoynt and constitute Deputies within the sayd Shiere, as well within liberties as without; and further by the same Commissione did geue vnto the sayd Deputies so by me to be appoynted and assygned, full power and authority in my absence to doo and execute in the sayd countie, all and every thinge and thinges by the sayd Commissione assygned and appoynted, by me to be done and executed: KNOWE YE THEREFORE, that I the sayd Sir Christopher Hatton, knight, haue, according to the tenor of the sayd Commissione, appoynted assygned and constituted my trusty and welbelouued [*sic*] Sir Jhon Spenser, Sir Rychard Knyghtley and Sir Edward Mountagewe, knightes, to be my Deputies in the sayd Countie of Northampton and all corporat and priuileged places within the lymites or precynctes of the sayd Countie.

And whatsoever the sayd Sir Jhon Spenser, Sir Rychard Knyghtley and Sir Edward Mountagewe, knyghtes, or any two of them shall doo or execute by force of the sayde Commissione within the sayde Countie of Northampton or within any corporat or priuileged place within the lymites or precynctes of the same, I, the sayde Sir Christopher Hatton, knyght, doo allowe and approue the same in all poyntes and in every thinge, as yf my self were present in persone.

In wytnes whereof, vnto these presentes I haue sett to my hand and seale. Dated the viijth of October, 1586, and in the eyght and twentith yeere of her Majesties reygne.

" CHR: HATTON "

[*fo.* 19b]   To the Right Worshipfull my assured good frendes, Sir Jhon Spencer, Sir Richard Knightley and Sir Edward Mountague, knightes.

[*Traces of Seal*]

9. [*fo.* 14a]   [LETTER. THE COUNCIL TO SIR CHRISTOPHER HATTON. 2 October, 1586.][1]

[*Copy. Enclosed with No. 7*]

After our ryght harty commendations. Where as her Majestie hath appoynted the number of one thousand men to be enrowled and redused vnder captaynes within that Countie, it is therefore thought convenient that you should make choyse of the pryncipall gentlemen of the Country, there knowen to be well affected in religione, to haue the leading of the foote men, appoynting to eche of the sayd gentlemen such nombers of men as to there places and qualities shall appertayne. Wherein it shalbe needefull and necessary to haue a care that the sayd nomber, considering they ar to be vsed for the gard of her Majesties persone, may (as neere

---

[1] Summarised in *M.B.S.*, p. 4.

as may be) consist of such househoulders as for their personage shalbe founde seruisable, and of lyving and hauiour able to beare the charge of the traynynge.

We also thinck convenient that, for the better traynynge of the sayde bandes, you should make choyce of some skilfull man to supply the place of muster master. And in case you shall fynde the inhabitantes of that Shire either vnwilling or vnable to beare the charges of the traynyng of the whole bandes, then we thinck it requisite, whereas it is appoynted in every band consisting of one hundred men there should be forty shott, twenty armed pykes and the rest furnished with bowes and billes according to the aptnes of those that shalbe enrowlled, that the sayd shott, amounting in the whole to the nomber of 400 according to this proportione, may be trayned by them selues without the rest.

Furthermore, to thende there may be some vniforme order obserued through out the Realme in the manner of traynyng the said footebandes, and to be performed with as litell charge to the country as may be, we haue thought good to send you herewith a coppie of the order obserued in the marityme Counties, to thende such as you shall appoynt to be muster master in that Countie may lykewyse follow the lyke dyrectiones in the forme of theire traynynge.

Now for the traynyng of the horsemen, we thinck it meete you should followe therein such orders and dyrectiones as we send you herewith, and ar sett downe for the rest of the Lieutenantes placed in the marityme Counties, where vnto we doo also referr you for all other matters, as for pyoners, carriages for seuerall bandes and for victualles, as also for the erecting and keeping of beacons.

And so we bidd you hartely fare well. From the Court at Wyndsor, the second of October, 1586.

Your lovinge frendes,

JHON CANTUAR   W. BURGHLEY   G. SHREWSBURY   H. DERBY
C. HOWARD   HUNSDON   JEAMES CROFT   F. WALSINGHAM
                 W. DAUISON   J. WOLLEY

[fo. 21b] A Coppie of the Lordes letters to Mr. Vicechamberlayne, her Majesties Lieutenant of the Countie of Northampton.

10. [fo. 26a] ORDERS TO BE OBSERUED BY THE LORDES LIEUTENANTES. [June, 1585.][1]

[Enclosed with No. 7]

First, to take order for the publishing of the Commissione.

To geue dyrectione for the mustering and exercising in martiall feates, such as were or shalbe trayned and reduced to bandes.

To cause a generall viewe to be taken of the able men within there seuerall

[1] Also in M.B.S., pp. 4-5.

charges, and to see how many of them may be armed with such armour as is presently to be had in the seuerall Counties within the saide charges.

To take a vewe of the horsemen and to appoynt captaynes ouer them, allotting to every captayne or coronell 50 horses with there seuerall cornettes, and to be clad with cassockes of one coullour.

To make choyse of a certayne nomber of pyoners.

To appoynt certayne carriages for victualles and other necessary thinges for every one of the sayde bandes, as also carriages for the pyoners.

To take order that there may be 300 or 400 shott sett vppon ordynary nagges or horse back.

To moue the Justices of the Peace that euery Justice of the Quorum may yeld to fynde two poytrynalles on horseback, and the other Justices that ar not of the Quorum one poytrynall on ordynary geldinges, to attend vppon the Lieutenant, to be clad in cassockes of one coullour at the charges of the sayd Justices, and to be ledd by some such captayne as by the sayde Lieutenant shalbe thought meete.

To see the beacons erected and well kept.

That espetiall care be had to discerne all papistes and other suspected persones.

It shalbe also necessary that an othe be mynistred, as well to the trayned souldiers as to the captaynes.

That such as are fermours and owners be enrolled (as neere as may be) in the trayned bandes.

To see that the pryuileged townes may alwayes haue a portione of powder in stoare, which shalbe delyuered them at the Quenes pryce.

[*fo.* 3lb]   Orders to be obserued by the Lieutenantes.

11. [*fo.* 27a]   Dyrectiones for the Corporalles. [July, 1585.][1]

[Enclosed with No. 7]

That for every corporall there may be a butt of xx*tie* foote broade and sixtene foote hygh, erected in some convenient place remote from the hygh way or other common frequented place, and in the middest thereof to sett a rundell of boorde of a yard and a half broade, with certayne black rundelles and a whyte in the middest, agaynst which the souldyer is to leuell his peece for his better ayme and ready discharginge.

That the souldier be placed 150 paces from the sayd butt and instructed how to stand comely in his peece, and that he fynde his marck readily thorowe the syght of his peece, and to knowe how to bryng the pyn standing vppon the mouth of his peece, his marck and syght of his peece, all into one dyrect lyne.

That every souldier shalbe lymited by the sayd corporall how many shott he shall discharge, aboue which nomber he may not shoote.

---

[1] Printed in *M.B.S.*, p. 7 as an addition to " Heades of Instructions for our Mustar Master ". See also *ibid.*, p. lviii. See **41** for another copy.

12. [*fo.* 28a] THE HEADES OF INSTRUCTIONS FOR A MUSTER MASTER. [September, 1586.][1]

[Enclosed with No. 7]

[*fo.* 29b] The heades of Instructions for a muster master.

13. [*fo.* 22a] THE ANCIENT PLACES WHER BECONS HAVE BEEN SETT. [1586]

Daventry, Dodington, Tychmarche, [Grat[d]], Vfforde, Gratton.

14. [*fo.* 23b]. THE AUNCIENT PLACES WHER BEACONS HAUE BYNE SETT. [1586]

Daventre, Dodington, Titchemarshe, Vfforde, Gratton.

15. [*fo.* 12b] THE AUNCIENT ORDER FOR BEACONS. [1586][2]

Inprimis, beacons to be made in places accustomed and that Tychemershe beacon be sett at Tychemershe churche steple, Dodington at Ecton steple, and Daventrie in Brynton steple, vnless the high constables canne advertise the Justices of a fytt steple. [*In the margin here:* Daventry, Dodington, Tychemershe, Gretton, Vfforde in Burrowe Soke, Brington.]

Item, a commaundement from the Sheriff and Justices to be made to the high constables of suche hundredes wheare the above named beacons stande, that they with all conuenyent expedicion cause those beacons [stande[d]] to be repayred that nede reparacions, and to make newe yf nede be, yf any of those be decayed, and to prepare barrells, lynkes and other necessaries for the same purpose, for whiche entyre charges they shall have vpon their billes exhibyted full allowaunce.

Item, that there be fower substanciall honest persons appoynted by the Justices of that dyvision or hundred wheare the seuerall beacons stande, to watche the same, viz: twoo by daye and twoo by night, whoe shall have for their wages viii*d.* a peece for the daye and the night.

And yf any of them discerne by daye or night any fyre, that with all expedicion they gyve warninge to the constables of the same towne to thentent that they forthwith maye repaire by daye or by nyght to twoo of the next Justices to gyve them knowledge therof, and that there be no beacon fyred vntill twoo of the Justices at the leaste come to the same place, and that the lynkes, barrells and suche other thinges as are to be sett on fyre shall be in the safe custody of the constable or other substanciallest person in that towne wheare the beacon standeth vntill the comynge of the Justices.

Item, for and towardes the makinge and reparacions of the said seuerall beacons, and the necessarie stuff therto apperteyninge, as also

¹ See **6** for another copy. ² Also in *M.B.S.,* pp. 7-8.

for the dayly and nightly wages of the watchers of the said beacons, it ys ordered that euery lorde within the County of Northampton [shall pay (?)] x*s.*; euery knight, vi*s.* viij*d.*; every esquyer, v*s.*; every gentleman, iij*s.* iiij*d.*; euery other substanciall honest yeoman, ij*s.*; and of euery man sett at x *li.* in the last subsedy, xij*d.*; and euery other sett at v *li.*,—vi*d.*

Item, for the oversight of the diligent watchinge by the watchers of the beacon of ECTON, Mr. Catisby, Mr. Rowse and Christofer Lewys and William Nycolles to be appoynted.

To BRINGTON, Robert Saunders, William Tanfeilde and William Gent.

To TYCHEMERSHE, William Dudley, Mr. Lenton, Gilberte Pyckering, John Pyckeringe.

To VFFORDE, Roberte Wyngfeilde, Roberte Browne, Frauncys Quarles, Arth[ur] Turnour.

To ROCKINGHAM, Edwarde Watson, William Palmer, Laurence Maydwell, Robert Chapman.

Item, that those Justices whosoever shall have knowledge by the constables of the fyringe of any other beacon, that they, after their repaire to the beacon they be charged with, cause not the same to be sett of fyre before they have intellygence by a spedy and trustie messenger of the cause why the fyred beacon was sett of fyre.

Item, that euery Justice or Justices within their seuerall dyvysyons shall dyrect their letters to the constables and fower of the substanciallest men of euery towne, that they and euery of them be circumspect and hedefull that none of the towne shall wander vpp and downe, nor runne abrode or sturre to the beacon fyred (yf any happen to be), but suche as shall be commaunded by the Justices or fower.

16. [*fo.* 22b] THE NAMES OF CERTEN GENTLEMEN THAT BE DEAD AND GONE WITHIN OUR COUNTY, &c., 1586.

Sir William Fy[tz]williams, Sir John Spencer, John Lane of Wolgrave, the Lady Margret Zouche, Edward Andrews, Laurance Maidwell, Michell Lues, Edward Barnwell, George Farmor, Roger Cave, Thomas Lovett, George Carlton, Edw. Onlye, Thomas Willmore, John Wake, Thomas Catesbye, Thomas Furthoe, Fraunces Sanders, Randall Ondale [*for* Goodall], Renold Braye, Sanwell [*sic*] Davers [*sic, for* Danvers], George Yorke, Thomas Marmion, Gerom. Farmor, Mrs. Tanfilde.

17. [*fo.* 22a] HONORABLE AND NOBLE PERS[O]N[A]GES NOT CHARGED BY VS. [1586?]

The [My^d] Lord Tresorer, the [my^d] Lord Bushop of Petborowe; the [my^d] Lord Zouche; the [my^d] Lord Vauxe; the [my^d] Lord Mordant; Sir Xpofer Hatton; Sir Walter Mildmay; Sir Tho. Sytcell [*for* Cecil]. Over and besides the number of gentlemen that be dead and gone, xxti.

18. [*fo.* 24a] Honorable and Noble Personages not Charged by vs. [1586?]

The Lord Treasurer [Lord Burghley], the Lord Bishoppe of Peterbrough, the Lord Zowche, the Lord Vauxe, the Lord Mordante, Sir Christopher Hatton, Sir Walter Myldmay, Sir Thomas Syssell.

Over and besides the nombre of gentell men that be deade and gone and in service for the prince in the said Countie:—xx*tie*.

19. [*fo.* 22a] The Names of the Captains for Horsmen and Footmen for the Conty of Northampton. [1586][1]

Capitans for the horsmen:
Ed. Griffin, Ed. Sanders [*these two names are bracketed*], John Stafforde, Mr. Chitwood, Esuby Isham, Edw. Montague, William Brown, Will. Dormor, Toby Chauncy, Tho. Burneby, John Read, John Elmes, Gi[l]bert Pikeringe, Tho. Catesby.
[*In the margin, opposite these names:*] Muster Master: Ed. Watson.

20. [*fo.* 22a] The Towns Priviliged Charged with Powder. [1586?][2]

Peterbroughe 1 pondes [50 pounds]; Northampton iij^c waghte [3 hundred weight]; Daventry, j^c waight; Ondell 1 *li.*; Ketheringe, 1 *li.*; Toceter, 1 *li.*; Wellingbrorowhe, 1 *li.*

21. [*fo.* 23b] The Names of the Captaines for the Horsemen and Footemen. [1586]

Edward Griffine [and] Edward Saunders, esquires, captaines of the horsemen.
John Stafford, [*blank*] Chitwood, Eusabie Ishame, Edward Mountague, Willm. Browne, William Darmor, Tobie Chauncie, Thomas Burnabie, John Rede, John Elmes, Gilbert Pyckeringe, Thomas Catesbie.

22. [*fo.* 23b] The Townes Charged with Powder. [1586?][3]

23. [*fo.* 75a] The Trial of Mary Queen of Scots. 15 October, 1586.][4]
Die Veneris fourteeneth [*sic*] die mensis Octobris, Anno Dommini 1586, infra Castrum de Fothryngaye actum per Commission:

[1] Also in *M.B.S.*, p. 9, where Chitwood's Christian name is given as Richard.
[2] Also in *ibid.*, where Brackley has been added. Cf. the list in Appendix 5.
[3] This list duplicates **20**.
[4] Lord Chancellor Bromley's speech and Queen Mary's protest were in fact made on Wednesday, 15 October. For an abbreviated version of the text of this document see T. B. Howell, *State Trials* (1816), i. 1173.

The Commissioners and Scottish Queene beinge all assembled and sett in her Majesties Chamber of Presence within the Castle of Forthringaie, the Lord Chauncellour deliuered that her Majestie, beinge strongelie enformed to her great sorrowe and greif that the destruction of her person and ouerthrow of her state hathe beene lately practised by the Scottish Queene, and findinge that notwithstanding her Majestes longe tolleracion of her inpatience the said Scottishe Queene conteinued her evill offence and was made the disturber of religion and of the common peace of this lande and other partes beyonde the seas; her Majestie had nowe for necessarie pollicy, as bounde therto by her principall office, commaunded this Assemblie for the examinacion therof, nor for malice, nor in regard of her owne persone (whome God woulde defende), but leaste if the Scottishe Queene weare faultie of the thinge mentioned in the Commission, and her Maiestye should be [so[f]] remised as suffer it to goe vnexamined, shee shoulde committe a great offence towardes God, forget her prouidence and beare the sworde in vayne. And therfore her Majestie had directed forth this Comission, vpon the readinge whereof and hearinge of theis matters which shoulde be deliuered by her Majesties learned Councell, the Scottish Queene should bee harde at large to speake what shee coulde in defence of her self or to declare her inocencie.

Herevpon the Scottish Queene, sainge that shee came into this lande for succour and vpon promis of release, and as noe subiecte, but was detayned as a prisoner, publiquelie and openlie protested that shee is an absolute and free princes, not acknowledginge any superior but God alone, and therefore shee desireth that before all other proceedinges it may be enacted that what soeuer shee shall doe in aunswearinge here before the Comissioners of the Queene of England her good sister, whome shee tooke to bee vntrewellye informed againste her, it may not be preiudiciall to her self, to the Princes her allies, nor to the Kinge her sonne, nor to anye that shall succeede her; which protestacion shee doeth not make as she saieth in regard of her own lief or to avoide the hearinge of the matter, but for the necessarie preseruacion of her prerogative, honor and dignitie. Not meaninge, as shee saieth, by this her appearance before [the] Comissioners to comprise or conclude her self as a subiecte to the Queene of England, but only entendinge thereby to dischardge her self and, by aunswearinge, to make it knowne to all the worlde that shee is not guilty to that haynous crime against her Majestes person with which shee seemed to be chardged, to which pointe onlie and to noe other shee will aunsweare, as shee saieth, and to none other. And this protestacion shee desireth to be had in continuall remembrance and a publique acte to be made therof, and the noble men and others here present to bee witnesses of this her protestacion, and then shee protesteth before the lyuinge God that shee loued the Queene as her dearest and eldeste sister, and had borne allwaies good will to this Countrie.

To these protestacions of the Scottish Queene, the Lord Chauncellour [not(?)] agnizinge[1] anye such her entraunce into the realme vpon promis from her Majestie, but disavowinge the same, replyinge openly and saithe that thoughe such protestacions weare of noe importaunce, because that shee beinge here within the realme chardged with the crime of that nature,

---

[1] Agnise = acknowledge.

of what estate soeuer shee weare shee became subiecte to the lawe, yet the Comissioners weare contented that her protestacions should bee entred onlie without anye approbate acceptaunce or allowance thereof by them; in the name of whome the Lord Chauncellour did then protest that the said protestacion of the Scottish Queene was a thinge mearlie voide and of noe effecte in lawe, and protested alsoe that her said pretended protestacion should not be in anye sorte preiudiciall to the dignity and suppreame power of our Soueraigne the Queenes Majeste nor to the prerogatiue of her Crowne, nor to the absolute iurisdiccion of the same or [of^d] [to^i] anye other priveledge apperteininge or incydente by any meanes to the Crowne of her Realme, nor to anye lawes therof, which protestacion the said Lorde Chauncellour in the name of [all^i] her Majestes Commissioners there present required alsoe to be entred and all persons presente to beare witnes thereof.

24. [fo. 23a]   MEN VEWED IN THE WESTE DEVICION.[1]

Anno Domini 1586, et anno regni Elizabeth regine xxviij.

NORTHAMPTON TOWNE: ij^C xxxiiij° [for 234], mustered at Northampton the first of Nouembre.

HUNDREDES of CLELEY, j^C xlti [140]; NORTON: j^C xxxti [130]; TOWCESTER: j^C ix. [109]
Somma: iij^C lxxix [379] mustered at Towcester the iij° of Nouembre.

HUNDREDS of SPELLOY: j^Clti [150]; WYMERSLEY: Clxxx [180]; NOBOTTEELL: ij^Ciiij° [204];
Somma: v^C xxxiiij°, mustered at Northampton on the ij° of Nouembre.

HUNDREDS of SUTTON: ij^Clx [260]; WARDEN; j^Cxxvj^ti (126).
Somma: iij^C lxxxvj, mustered at Culworth the iiij° of Nouembre.

HUNDREDS of FAWESLEY: ij^Cxx^ti [220]; GUYLSBOROUGH: iii^Cx [310].
Somma: v^Cxxx^ti [530], mustered at Dauentre the fyfte of Nouembre.
Somma totalis: ij^Mlxiij [2063].

In the HUNDREDS of CLELEY: corsletes [blank], caliuers [blank]; NORTON: corseletes [blank], caliuers [blank]; TAWCESTER, corslets [blank], caliuers [blank].

In the HUNDREDS of SPELLOE: corslets [blank], caliuers [blank]; WYMERSLER [sic]: corslets [blank], caliuers [blank]; NOBOTTELL: corslets [blank], caliuers [blank].

In the HUNDREDS of SUTTON: corslets [blank], caliuers [blank]; WARDEN: corslets [blank], caliuers [blank].

---

[1] Also in M.B.S., pp. 9-10.

In the HUNDREDS of FAWSLEY: corsletes [blank], caliuers [blank]; GUYLESBOROUGH: corsletes [blank], caliuers [blank].

Somma totalis of theis corsletes: ij^cj [for 201]; of the calliuers: lxxxviij [88].

---

25. [fo. 53a] [LETTER. THE MAYOR, JUSTICES OF THE PEACE AND ALDERMEN OF NORTHAMPTON TO SIR CHRISTOPHER HATTON AND SIR WALTER MILDMAY. 4 November, 1586.]

Righte honourable, our bounden dewties most humblie remembred. Yt maye please you tonderstand that wee, the Maior, Justices and Aldermen of the towne of Northampton, haue receyued a most pyttifull complaynte and supplication vnder the handes of three hvndreth [of] thynhabitauntes and poore people of our towne, conteyninge the same effecte that this vnto your Honoures doth.

And forsamvch as we doe thinke and are fullie perswaded that ether all or the moste parte thereof ys verye trewe, we therefore doe most earnestlie desire your Honoures helpes for the reformacion of suche maulsters, regraters, and ingrossers of corne, and suche an vnnecessarye nombre of kylles[1] whereby our poore people are so hardlie distressed that we stand in great dowte of some mvtenie or vnlawfull attempte to aryse amongeste them, vnles somme politique meanes be devised for the spedye reformacion of suche horrible abuses, which the Lorde God graunte at his good will and pleasure.

Northampton, the iiiith of November, 1586.

Your Honours most bounden,

"JOHN BECHINO [for BICHENO] MAIOR" "JOHN BALGAY"
"JOHN LONG" "JOHN BRYAN" "JOHN HENSMAN"
"THOMAS PEMARTON"

[fo. 57b] To the Righte Honorable and our esspeciall good frendes, Sir Christofer Hatton and Sir Walter Myldmaye Knyghtes, beinge of her Majesties Priuie Counsell, geue these.

---

26. [fo. 17a] [LETTER. THE COUNCIL TO THE SHERIFF OF NORTHAMPTONSHIRE (BARTHOLOMEW TATE[2]). 6 November, 1586.]

After our hartie commendacions. Whereas her Majestie is enformed that of late years diuers in that Cowntie haue brought in an vse to feede and fatt their sheepe with peaze, which maketh the flesh both vnsauerie and vnholsome, forasmoch as in the time of dearth of other graine by the vnseasonablenes of these latter yeares, all manner of graine[3] beinge both scarcer, and growne to so excessiue prices as the abilitie of the poore

---

[1] Kilns, for making malt.
[2] Tate was sheriff until 14 November.
[3] At this period "graine" commonly signified peas and beans as well as corn.

Righte honorable our bounden deuties most humble remembred. yt maye please
you tounderstand that wee the Maior, Justices and Aldermen of the Towne of
Northampton haue receyued a most pyttifull complaynte, and supplication vnder
the handes of three hondreth thynhabitantes and poore people of our towne,
conteyninge the same effecte that this vnto your honores doth; and forasmuch
as we doe thinke, and are fullie perswaded, that either all or the most parte thereof
ys verye trewe: wee therefore doe most earnestlie desire your honores helpes
for the reformaton of suche Maultsters, regraters, & ingrossers of corne,
and suche an vnnecessarye nombre of Alehowses, whereby our poore people are
so hardlie distressed that we stand in great dowte of some mvtenie or
vnlawfull attempte to aryse amongeste them, vnles some politique meanes be
deuised for the spedye reformaton of suche horrible abuses: which the
Lorde god graunte at his good will and pleasure. / Northampton the
iiijth of Nouember. 1586

    your honores most bounden .

        John Rogino maior
                Lyes Spalbray
        John Cowl / John Bryan .
        John Consinan

            Thomas pomayton

LETTER FROM MAYOR, J.P.S AND ALDERMEN OF NORTHAMPTON TO
HATTON AND MILDMAY (No. 25)

is not able to afforde them breade corne, and neuerthelesse the season hath yelded good quantitie of peaze; her Majestie, havinge verie especiall care for the releefe and sustentacion of the poore people, consideringe the scarcitie of corne and beinge geuen to vnderstand of this kinde of feedinge of sheepe latelie taken vp with that graine which might supplie the necessitie of the poorer sorte in this time of dearth, hath geuen expresse charge and commaundement vnto vs to signifie her will and pleasure vnto yow by these our letters, whereby yow are authorised in her name (callinge vnto yow some of the Justices of the Peace of that Cowntie with their advice) to take generall order thorowe out that Sheere, that from henceforth there maie no sheepe be fatted or fedd with that kinde of graine, which they shall forbeare to doe as they will be loth to incurre her Majesties displeasure and awnswere the contrarie at their perils.

And to the end notice maie be geuen hereof to the whole Cowntie, yow shall cause this her Majesties pleasure to be published in euery market towne, wherein (not withstandinge this inhibicion) if anie shall, in contempt of this her Highnes pleasure or proceedinge tendinge to a publicke benefit, emploie that graine to soch vse as hereby is forbidden, yow shall, vppon informacion geuen yow thereof, take bondes of the parties so offendinge to make their personall apparence here before vs, to awnswere their contempt in that behalfe.

So fare yow well. From Richmond, the 6th of November, 1586,

Your lovinge freindes,

" Jo : Cant. " " T. Bromley, Canc. " " W. Burghley "
" H. Derby " " C. Howard " " H. Hunsdon " " W. Cobham "
" T. Buckehurst " " Northampton " " Chr : Hatton " " J. Wolley "

[*Traces of seal*]

[*fo.* 18b] To our verie loving freinde, the Shir[rif]f of the Countie of Northampton for the time beinge. Northampton.

27. [*fo.* 52a] [Letter. The Council to Knightley, Montagu, Bartholomew Tate and Francis Barnard. 30 November, 1586.][1]

After our hartie commendacions. Wee are giuen to vnderstande of diuers gre[ate] disorders commonlie practized of late, in rasing the m[ar]kettes and price of kindes of corne in the saide towne [of Northamton[*i*]] to the greate discommoditie and distr[esse] of the moste parte of the inhabitantes thereof. Wee haue therefore th[oughte] it verie requisite, for reformacion of these abuses and for the comf[orte] and releefe of the poorer sorte of the said towne in this time of de[arthe], to requier you,[2] and by vertue hereof to authorize you, to take presente

---

[1] The outside edge of fo. 52 has perished. One or two words and the ends of others have been conjecturally supplied in square brackets.

[2] Knightley and Montagu were chosen for this task because they were deputy lieutenants; Tate and Barnard, because they were J.P.s residing near Northampton.

[order] in that behalfe in suche sorte as hereafter followeth :-

First, you shall searche and enquier whoe they be that are the grea[te] engrosers of corne as, by buying the same groweing on the gr[ound] or els by laying out their monyes aforehande, gett into their ha[ndes] the whole croppes of manie poore men, so as the marketes cann[ot] be so orderlie serued and the poore thereby sustained as before tym[e] they haue ben.

Item, you ar to searche out whoe they be of that towne which ar poss[es]sioners and farmors of manie parsonages and tithes and impropriacions, whereby it is like they maie haue muche corne in store.

Item, whoe they be that are the forestallers and regrators of the markettes, and to peruse also their stoare.

You must likewise take order that the markett be not troubled, hindred or annoyed in anie sorte by badgers.

This being don, you shall searche the barnes, granars and storehou[ses] of the foresaide parties inhabiting with in the towne of Northampton [and] within three or fower miles of to the same towne. And whe[n] you shall haue considered of their necessarie expences in their owne howses of all kindes of their saide corne and sufficient [for] their seede, etc., you shall apporcion the same which remaineth and [take] bondes of the parties to serue the market therewith euerie market daie, rate[ably] by euen porcions at suche reasonable prices as the market th[en] yeeldeth, and not to buie them selues anie corne in that marke[t] or other where during this time of dearth, but to vse and liue vp[on] their owne, as is aforesaide.

You shall likewise take paines to view all the kylles now built within that towne for mault, and cause so manie of the said how[ses] to be converted in other vses as in your discrecions, for the danger of fier or annoyance of the towne or neighbourhoode, or anie oth[er] thing preiudiciall in the inhabitantes, shalbe thoughte meete.

[*In left hand margin here at foot of fo. 52a, in another hand* :-] Sir Richard Knightlie, Sir Edward Mountagu, Bartho : Tate, [*blank*] Barnarde of Abing[ton].

And if you shall finde anie of them that you shall deale with in theis causes not content to submitt them selues and to obserue and obey suche orders as you shall herein set downe vnto them, you shall then immediatlie certefie vs of their names and take good and substanciall bandes of them to her Majesties vse, that they appere before vs within tenn daies then next ensuinge, etc.

Wee haue herewith sent you the peticion enclosed, whereby you maie the better see their complaintes of their owne greefes to the which we referr you, etc.

Thus not doubting of your carefullnes in the xecucion of theis our direccions for publike benefitt without anie priuate respect, wee byd you farewell. From Richemont, the xxxth. of Nouember, 1586.

Your verie louinge frendes,

"T. BROMLEY, Canc." "W. BURGHLEY" "CHR: HATTON" "FRA: WALSINGHAM" "W: DAUISON" "WA: MILDMAYE" "R. SADLEIR"

Sir Richard Knightlie
Sir Edward Mountagu
Bartho. Tate
[*Blank*] Barnarde of Abing[ton]

[*fo.* 58b] To our verie lovinge freindes, Sir Richard Knightlie, Sir Edward Mountagu, knightes, Bartholomew Tate and [Mr*ⁱ*] Barnard, esqres.

[*Traces of seal*]

28. [*fo.* 55b] [PETITION. THE COMMONALTY OF NORTHAMPTON TO SIR CHRISTOPHER HATTON AND SIR WALTER MILDMAY. 1586.]

[*Enclosed with No. 27*]

Toe the Right Honorable Sir Chrystofer Hatton, knight, Vicechamberlane to her Majestie, and Sir Walter Myldmay, knight, her Highnes most honorable Counsellors.

Moste pyttifullie complayninge, shewe vnto your Honors thynhabytauntes of Northampton, that all manner of grayne ys nowe growne to suche an high price as wee are not able to maynteyne oure wyves, children, and famelies with nedefull bread.

And forasmuche as yt ys moste apparent that thys inconvenience commeth most cheiflie bye the multitude of maulsters and regraters of corne within oure [towne*ⁱ*] and Countie of Northampton, but speciallie wythin oure towne and liberties, the same being (for the most parte) aldermen, bayliffes and men of great welthe, having verie good and rytche traydes to lyve otherwayes, who haue sett vppe to the nomber of sixtene kylles at the leest within the towne and liberties, and manye of them in most daungerous and fearfull places for burning the towne; and vnder the pretence and culloure of maultynge, and some of oure bakers vnder pretence of buying corne for theire trayde, doe gett into theire handes whole farmes [and] tythes of parsonages; some buye nedye mens corne vpon the grounde beforehand, and sell the same agayne bye tenne quarters to one man att one tyme, not within oure market, but to men of welth, sending yt abroade with cartes into the countrie, vsing all sinister and vnlawfull meanes to rayse a dearth and to bring a famine amongest the inferiors and poorest sort of people, which in oure towne are verie manye.

And although there be verie good lawes prouided for suche men, and that informars be contynuallie almost everie weeke amongest them, yett there ys not anye amendment, soe as yt ys toe be feared that thinformars are brybed, the lawes are broken, her Maiestie loseth her right, and the pore multitude of youre humble suppliauntes are like to be starved.

Whereuppon within fewe dayes now last past, wee haue exhibeted oure bill of complaynt to the worshipfull Mr. Bytchenoe, nowe Maior of oure towne, for hys assistaunce and hys brethren the Justices in thys oure great dystresse.

And most humblie (even casting oure selves downe before the feete of your Honors) with pyttifull teares, crye and crave for some good order and reformacion for oure releif in thys oure greate miserie, which yf yt shall please the Lord to putt into your hartes toe performe, there ys no dowt but that your Honors shall therebye not onlie prevent some greate inconvenience verie like to fall owte amongest vs, but alsoe bynd the whole bodye of thys towne to praye for your Honors, even during oure lyves.

Your Honoures pore and most humble suppliantes,

THE COMINALTIE OF THE TOWNE OF NORTHAMPTON.[1]

Marke Robines, Will'm Danbie, Edward Langham, Richard Browne, Richard Storer, Will'm Crosse, Nicholas Witsey, Will'm Whellowes, George Foxe, Richard Bradshawe, Edward Lechefeild, Henrie Chawnor, John Lyncowne, Rycharde Twygden, Edwarde Hunter, Anthonie Walker, John Hatter, Hewghe Mores, Richard Wattes.[2]

Wyllyame Harpoll, Richard Wattes,[2] Henry Goodall, Richard Potter, Thomas Harris, Wyll'm Clavell, Thomas Potter, Thomas Judkyns, John Nellson, Xpofer Martin, Richard Marryatt, Henry Hollys, John Dombleston, Edward Armentage, John Brafeilde, Thomas Mercer, Will'm Corbett, Will'm Holland, Richard Elsey.

Henry Greene, Anthony Oldman, Chrystofer Hodshkyns, Will'm Wodd, James Wylkynson, Mark Robyns, Will'm Samwell, John Shingleton, Nicholas Long, Henrie Stubbes, Will'm Sparreman, Rob't Hatter, Anthonie Browne, John Hatton, Nicholas Parker.

John Greneway, Robert Lee, Robert Fyssher, Edward Langham, George Andrew, Peter Pytman, Wyll'm Nutt, Henrie Trott, Fraunces Howmes, John Burwell, John Howmes, John Heyward, Francis Bott, Roberte Parker, Richard Pryce.

29. [fo. 62a] [THE NAMES OF PERSONS SELLING MALT. December, 1586?]

The Names of those that have made Former Bargens, &c.

John Kirtlande hathe to delyver to one of Coventrye, ij quarters of malt.

John Hainsworth hathe to delyver to Hiltons wief of Daventrye, v quarters of malte.

Lauraunce Marche hathe to delyver to Thomas Lovet, salter of Nantwiche, x quarters of malt.

Thomas Humfrey hathe to delyver to one Banester, a Lankeshier man, v strick malte.

And more is ther not bargend of anie of these.

---

[1] The names following, which are not autographs, are written in four columns, here represented by separate paragraphs.
[2] There were evidently two men of this name—father and son—resident in Northampton at this time. See J. C. Cox, *The Records of the Borough of Northampton* (1898), ii. 153.

30. [*fo.* 59a] [NOTE OF A RECOGNIZANCE CONCERNING DEARTH OF GRAIN IN NORTHAMPTON. December, 1586?]

Anno Domini 1586. The Recognisaunce for the Men of Northampton.

The condition of this recognisaunce is suche that if the said A.B. or anie person to his vse shall not by anie weise or meanis whatsoever from the xiijth daie of December last paste, during the tyme of this dearth, buy anie barly to malte, or anie other kinde of green [grain] more then shall conveniently suffice his owne family to feed vpon, and also that he shall sell no manner of grayn out of this markett, and especially that the town of Northampton may be first served therwith, that then this present recognisaunce to be void and of none effecte, or otherwies to stand and remayn in his full power and efficacy, &c.

THE NAMS OF ALL THOSE THAT HAVE ACKNOLEGED THIS RECOGNISAUNCE

John Mercer, glover; Will'm Rainsforde, baker, not restrainde to buy corne for his trad of bakinge; John Kirtlande, gent.; John Hainswort, glover; Laurance Marshe, yoman; Roger Hasket of Cotton End; John Green, malster; Bartlemewe Johnson, malster; Thomas Humfrey, draper; Walter Kirtlande, maltster; John Hopkens, mercer, bonde for vidua Hopkens; Thomas Adams, bachelor; Abraham Ventris, maltster.

Eche of thes in one hundred pounde a pece, to the vse of her Majestie, for performance of the condition abousade.

31. [*fo.* 54a] [LETTER. THE COUNCIL TO HATTON AND SIR WALTER MILDMAY. 7 January, 1586/7.]

[Copy. Enclosed with No. 32]

After our hartie commendacions. The Queenes Majestie, vnderstanding the greate dearth and scarcitie of all manner of graine and other victuall generallie within most partes of the Realme, bothe by vnseasonablenes of theis latter yeares and also by the vncharitable holding vp of prices by corne ma[ul]sters and ingrossers of [corne^d], graine and other victualls, hath of her princelie care she hath of the relieffe of her good and lovinge subiectes, speciallie such [are^d] as are poore and not able to endure the continuance of the present dearthe, commaunded us to thinke vppon some good meanes wherbie the markettes might be better served and the poore releived, on whom this burden doth lighte most heavelie in some parte.

Wherevppon we have devised theis orders[1] which you shall receave herewithall, which we hope through Godes goodnes shall breede greate ease to the pore pleple [*sic*], if you will performe your duties to see the same duelie and throughlie executed. Wherevnto we are vearie earnestlie and in her Majesties name to will and charge you to vse all care, diligence

[1] See **33.**

and requisitt traveill to see the same in all pointes loked vnto and observed; wherein you shall doe a thinge vearie acceptable to her Majestie, of greate charitie to your neighbours, and worthie of your place and callinges.

And so we bid you hartielie farewell. From the Courte at Grenewiche, the vijth of Januarie, 1586.

T. BROMLEY, Canc.   W. BURLEIGH   H. DARBIE   W. COBHAM
T. BUCKEHURST   JAMES CROFT   CHR. HATTON   J. WOLLY

Northampton

32. [*fo.* 60a]   [LETTER. THOMAS ANDREW, SHERIFF, TO KNIGHTLEY. 11 January, 1586/7.]

Right Worshipfull, hauing receaved letters from my Lordes of the Queenes Maiestyes most honorable Counsell for orders to be taken for the releife and stay of the present dearth of graine within this County, with a booke of orders sett downe in print very long to copy out, the copy of wich letters with a breviatt of the sayd orders[1] you shall receive hereinclosed, desyring you and Sir Edward Mountague, according to the sayd order, to agre of some convenient day presently of meting at Northampton within this fyve or six dayes, that the rest of the Justices may likewise have spedy warning to be there, for that their absence without necessarye cause is to be considered of.

Thus with my harty commendacions, I comytt you to the Allmighty. Charwelton, the xith of January, 1586.

                    " Yowers to commande,
                         THO. ANDREWE "[2]

[*fo.* 61b]   To the Right Worshipfull Sir Richard Knightley, knight, yeive these.

[*Traces of seal*]

33. [*fo.* 60b]   [A BREVIATT OF THE] ORDERS DEVISED BY THE ESPECIALL COMAUNDMENT OF THE QUEENES MAJESTIE FOR THE RELEIF AND STAY OF THE PRESENT DEARTH OF GRAINE WITHIN THE REALME. [January, 1586/7.][3]

[Enclosed with No. 32]

1. That the Justices shall devide them selves into sundry partes to execute theis orders.

[1] See **33** and note. On fos. 60 and 61, forming one sheet, is Andrew's letter, and overleaf (on fos. 60b and 61a) is the " breviatt " of the Queen's orders referred to in his letter, the direction to Knightley being on fo. 61b.
[2] " Yowers to commande " is in the same hand as the signature.
[3] This is a " breviatt " of the Orders drawn up on 27 Dec. 1586, printed in E. M. Leonard, *The Early History of English Poor Relief* (Cambridge, 1900), pp. 319-26.

2. To apoint sundry juries to enquyre of thinges hereafter following.

3. The oth of the jurors with chardg to enquyre what nomber of persons be in the houses of them that have stoore of corne.

4. For badgers, broggers and caryers of corne.

5. Maltmakers, bakers and brewers.

6. Buyers of corne to sell againe.

7. Buyers of corne vpon the ground.

8. Against such as shall refuse to declare the truth of the matters inquirable.

9. Partyes offending to appere afore the Counsell.

10. A consideracion of all persons that have corne, to determyne howe they shall serve the markettes with such portions as they may spare.

11. The forme of the recognizaunce to be frely taken.

12. Orders to be observed by such as shall be apointed to serve the markettes with corne for the releife of the poore people first.

13. To whom corne shall be sold after that the poore are served.

14. Noe corne brought to the markett vnsold to be caryed out of the towne.

15. None to buy such kind of corne as they shall bring to sell but by warraunt vpon reasonable causes.

16. Noe corne to be bowght for to sell againe.

17. Noe corne to be bowght but in open markett.

18. Enquyrye to be made against ingrossers.

19. An order for all licences from the Justices of the Peace to be kept in a record.

20. Regard to the bakers for keping of the syse of bread.

21. Bread faulty in any excesse to be sold towardes the releif of the poore.

22. Noe badger to buy corne but in open markett, and with a sufficient licence in writinge.

23. The badgers to shewe weekly ther bookes of buying.

24. Noe Justices servant to be a badger, nor none other but such as be licensed in open Sessions.

25. Noe badger, baker, brewer or purveyer to buy graine vntill an howre after the full markett begynns.

26. Some Justices to be present in the markett to see the poore releived vpon reasonable pryces.

27. Where Justices are wanting in any Hundred for to apoint some rich persons to supply the want.

28. That ministers and prechers exhort the rich sort to be iiberall to help the more with mony or victuall nedfull.

29. To make malt of otes in Countryes wher ther hath bene vse thereof.

30. Noe wast of bread corne superfluously, nor any expence therof but for feeding of people.

31. None suffered to make starch of any graine.

32. Able poore people to be sett to worke.

33. Stockes of mony for provision of workes for poore people.

34. Clothyers to continewe ther workefolkes.

35. Soldiers hurt and impotent people to be releived in ther dwelling places.

36. That noe myllers be suffered to be comon buyers of corne, nor to sell meale, but to attend to the trewe grynding of the corne brought, and to vse measurable toll theis deere seasons.

37. Conferences to be had betwixt the Justices of Peace in the Shyres and the principall officeres of cityes and townes corporate for provisions of graine for the enhabitantes in cityes and corporate townes.

38. Order for places exempted from the jurisdiction of the Justices of Peace in the bodyes of the Shires.

39. Regard to stay all transportacion of graine out of the Realme.

40. Certificat to be made of the execucion of these orders monthly to the Shreif, and he to certify the same to the Privy Counsell within [euery*d*] forty dayes.

41. To certify what Justices be absent from the service, that such as without iust excuse shall not attend, maye be displaced and the romes (yf ther be nede) supplyed.

34. [*fo.* 32a] [LETTER. LORD BURGHLEY, HATTON AND W. DAVISON TO KNIGHTLEY AND ANTONY COPE. 20 January, 1586/7.][1]

After our very hartie commendacions. Wheras we haue receaued some informacion that one John Arden of Elmely in the Countie of Northampton and his brother John Arden of Brackley in the same Countie are to be charged with the conspiracy of Ballard and Babington; theise are to requier you that immediatly vppon the receipt hereof you proceede to the apprehension of the said parties and searche of their howses for soche letters as haue passed betwen them and any others which may seame suspicious, puttinge their goodes and evidences in securitie vntill you shall receaue farther direction from vs. And the same persones, with soche or other writinges as may giue you cause of suspicious dealinge to be vsed by them, to sende vpp to vs, hauinge allwaies respect that the saide parties be kept asonder, without any meanes of conference or other intelligence.

And so we bidd you hartely farewell. At the Courte att Grenewich, the xxth of January, 1586.

Your louinge frendes,

" W. BURGHLEY "   " CHR: HATTON "   " W. DAUISON "

Sir Richard Knightley
Mr. Antony Cope

[*fo.* 37b] To our louving frendes, Sir Richard Knightley, knight, and Antony Cope, esquier.

[*A further endorsement:*] Ardens [*struck through*]

[*Traces of seal*]

---

[1] In the top left hand corner of this page is written " i3 ". See **35**, footnote

35. [*fo.* 33a] [LETTER. THE COUNCIL TO KNIGHTLEY AND ANTONY COPE. 30 January, 1586/7.][1]

After our hartie commendations. Ther is lately fallen out cause that mouith vs to think it very requisite that Thomas Arden, brother to John Arden of Elmneley, should be brought hither vnder safe custodie. We pray yow therfore to take order that he may be accordingly sent vp, as of late the other twoo Ardens were. For your trauell and carefullnes wherin, as we giue you our hartie thankes, so we will not omytt any fytt occasion to mak the same knowen to her Majestie.

And so we byd you hartely farewell. From Grenwich, the 30 of January, 1586.

Your loving frendes,

"Jo: CANT."   "H. DERBY"   "C. HOWARD"   "H. HUNSDON"
"W. COBHAM"   "T. BUCKEHURST"   "W. DAUISON"   "J. WOLLEY"

Postscr[ipt]. We require yow to examyn Henry Pedder vpon the flyeng of John Arden of Elmmeley, in what place and how farre from Pedders house he was found, and by what meanes.

Sir Richard Knightley
Anto. Cope

[*fo.* 36b] To our very loving frendes, Sir Richard Knightley, knight, and Antony Cope, esquiere.

[*Traces of seal*]

36. [*fo.* 74b] [A NOTE OF THE EXECUTION OF MARY QUEEN OF SCOTS ON 8 FEBRUARY, 1586/7.]

The viijth daie of Februar, 1586, in the xxixth yere of the Reign of the Queens Majestie that nowe is, ELIZABETH by the Grace of God, &c.

The Q[ueen] of Scotes was executed at the Castle of Fodringey, the daie and yere aboue said, in the Hall ther, wher was a scaffolde made of purpose for her execution.

The Comissioners apointed for the said execution was [*sic*] George, Earle of Shrewsb[ur]ye, Lord Marshall of England, the Earle of Kent, the Earle of Darby, the Earle of Cumberland, the Earle of Penbrocke.

To v, iiij, iij, or ij of them.

And the said Earles of Shrewsbery and Kent were ther, and no moe of them.

[*In another hand:*] Thomas Andrewe of Wynnwick, esquier, was then

---

[1] At the top left hand corner of the page is written "i4". This letter and that on fo. 34a (**38**) are in the same hand.

Shreif of this Countie of Northampton, whoe had chardge giuen him by thabousaid yearles to see thexecucion done.

Sir Amias Paulet hauinge then the keepinge of her in the Castle aforsaid, and against her death was appointed Sir Drue Drurye, knighte, and Mr. Roberte Beale, on of the Clearkes of her Majesties Counsell, [who] weare appointed to be there as asistaunce to Sir Amias Paulet.

Sir Richard Knightley and Sir Edward Mountague, Deputie Liftannantes of this Countie, weare alsoe appoynted to be there att her executition [*sic*].

37. [*fo.* 38a] [LETTER. HATTON TO KNIGHTLEY AND MONTAGU. 15 March, 1586/7.]

After my verie hartie commendacions. Whereas it hath pleased my Lordes of her Majesties Counsell to directe their letters vnto me as her Majesties Lieutenaunte of that Countie, to proceede to the due execucion of suche orders as ar nowe to be observed within the inlande counties of the Realme, for the trayning of suche number of men as ar to be leavied in everie Shiere according to former instruccions sett downe by their Lordships in that behalfe, I haue thowghte good for the better accomplishement of this service to sende herewith vnto yow (as her Majesties Deputie Lieutenauntes of that Shiere) the originall letter it selfe directed by their Lordships vnto me, to thende yow maye thereby vnderstande their particular direccions and pleasures signified to me therein.

As also earnestly to praye and requier yow to be verie carefull in the choice of men to be made, bothe of personable and hable bodies and suche as maye be thowghte serviceable in all other respectes, which, by the discreete care of your captains to be appoincted for that purpose, it is hoped maye be well and sufficiently performed; and that in your proceedinges yow haue an especiall regarde that the orders sett downe (the copies whereof I sende yow also herewith)[1] maye in everie poincte be duely and carefully observed, according to the truste reposed in yow, and the speciall charge committed in this behalfe to your vigilant care and circumspection.

Whereof not dowbting but yow will haue all good and due respecte bothe for your owne reputacions and myne, and her Majesties good opinion of the Shiere, I bidde yow verie hartiely fare well. From London, the xvth of Marche, 1586.

> Your verie loving assured frende,
> " CHR : HATTON "

Sir Richarde Knightley and Sir Edw : Mountague.

[*fo.* 43b] To the Right Worshipfull my verie good frendes, Sir Richarde Knightley and Sir Edwarde Mountague, knightes, her Majesties Deputy Lieutenauntes of the Countie of Northampton.

[*A hole in the paper to the right of the direction marks the place where the seal has been cut away.*]

---

[1] See **6**, **39**, **40**, and **41**.

38. [*fo.* 34a]   [LETTER. THE COUNCIL TO HATTON, 20 February, 1586/7.][1]

[Enclosed with No. 37]

After our hartie commendations. Wheras her Majestie hath appoynted the nomber of twelue hundred men to be enrolled and reduced vnder captens in that Countie of Northampton vnder your Lieutenancy, wherof iiij^C iiij^{xx} to be calyveres, ii^C xl^{ty} to be bowemen, ii^C xl^{ty} corslettes and ii^C xl^{ty} billes, it is therfore thought good that you should make choyce of the principall gentlemen of that Countie, there knowen to be well affected in religion, to haue the leading of the footemen, appoynting to eache of the sayd gentlemen such nombers of men as to their places and qualities shall appertayn, wherin it shall be nedefull and necessary to haue a care that the said nomber, considering they are to be vsed for the garde of her Majesties person, may (as neere as may be) consiste of such housholders as for their parsonnage shall be found seruicable, and of lyving and hauiour able to beare the charges of the trayning [of the said bandes^d]. We allso think convenyent that for the better trayning of the said bandes you should make choyce of som skillfull man to supply the place of muster master.

And in case you shall fynde the inhabitantes of the Sheir eyther vnwilling or vnable to beare the charges of the trayning of the wholle bandes, then we think it requisite that, wheras it is appoynted in euery band consisting of one hundred parsons there should be forty shott, twenty armid pykes and the rest to be furnished with bowes and billes according to the aptnes of those that be enrolled, that the said shott, amounting in the wholle to the nomber of 480 according to this proportion, may be trayned by themselves with out the rest.

Furthermore to the end ther may be som vniform order obseruid through the Realm in the manner of trayning of the said footbandes, and to be performid with as lyttle charge to the Country as may be, we haue thought good to send yow herewith a copie of the order obseruid in the maritime Counties, to the end such as you shall appoynte to be muster master in that Countie may lykewise followe the lyke directions in the form of their trayning.

And so we byd you very hartely farewell. From Grenwich, the xxth of February, 1586.

Your very assured loving frendes,

"Jo. CANT'"   "W. BURGHLEY"   "H. DERBY"   "C. HOWARD"
"H. HUNSDON"   "W. COBHAM"   "F. KNOLLYS"
"FRA. WALSINGHAM"   "J. WOLLEY"

To [my^d] Mr. Vice Chamberlen, Lieutenant of the County of Northt'.

---

[1] Summarised in *M.B.S.*, p. 9.

[*fo.* 35b] To our very loving frend, Sir Christofer Hatton, knight, her Majesties Vicechamberlen, one of her Majesties most honorable Priuie Counsell, and Lieutenant of the Countie of Northampton.

[*Further endorsements:*] Inl^d [*for* Inland] Mar. [*for* Maritime]

[*In margin:*] To Mr. Vicechamberlen.

39. [*fo.* 46a]   ORDERS TO BE OBSERUED BY THE LIEUETENANTS.[1]
[1586?]

[Enclosed with No. 37]

Inprimis, to cause a generall viewe to bee taken by their deputies of the able men within their seuerall charges, and to see how many of them maye bee armed with such armor as is presently in the seuerall Counties, within their said [County (?)] beesides the nomber appointed to bee trayned.

To take a view of the horsmen and to appoint captaines ouer them, allotting to everie captaine and cornet 50 horse, which severall cornetes are to bee clad with cassockes of one color.

To moove the Justices of Peace that everie Justice of Quorum may yeelde to finde 2 petronels on horsback, and the other Justices that are not of the Quorum, one petronell vpon ordinarie geldinges to attend vpon the Lieuetenantes, to bee all clad in cassockes at the charge of the Justices, and to bee ledd by some such captaines as by the said Lieutenant shalbee thought meet.

That such as are farmors or owners bee enrolled as neer[e] as may bee in the trained bandes, according to former instructions in anno 1584.

To see that the priuileged townes maie alwaies have a proportion of powder in store, which shalbee deliuered to them at the Queenes price.

[*fo.* 49b] Orders to bee obserued by the Lieuetenants of the inland Counties.
[*In another hand:*] For Mr. Vicechamberlin.

40. [*fo.* 44a] [AN ORDER FOR THE TRAINING OF SHOT. May, 1584. (*Copy*)][2]

[Enclosed with No. 37]

The leaders and captaines who are apointed to instruct and traine the shott shall cause an halbard to be sett vp in the plaine, wherby everie shott maie passe in that order which the French men call *a la file* and,

---

[1] Also in *M.B.S.*, pp. 10-11.
[2] Also in *ibid.*, p. 11. For the date of the document, see *ibid.*, p. lviii.

as wee terme it, in ranck as wild geese, and so passing by the halbard to present his peece and make offer as thoughe he would shoote. And those which doe not behaue them selves with their peeces as they ought maie receave particuler instruction and teaching. This exercise would be vsed twoe or three meetings at the least for ignorant people, in which time maie bee discerned those that cannot frame them selves in anie likelihood to proove shott, in whose roomes the captaines maie require others to bee placed who are more apt therevnto.

Afterwardes to teach them howe to hold their peeces from endangering them selves and their fellowes, to putt in them matches and to acquaint them with false fyres, by priming only the pan and not chardging the peece, which will envre the eye with the flash of the fyre, embolden the parties, and make everie thing familiar and readie vnto them. Then giue the peece half his chardge and acquaint them in skirmishing wise to come forward and retyre orderly againe; after to proceed to the full chardge; and lastly to the bullett, to shoote at a marke for some trifle to bee bestowed on him that best deserveth the same.

With this order and pollecie men shall in short time bee exercised, and with the xth part of the charges, to the great ease of the Contrie and saving of powder, for that in this maner it is found that two pound of powder will serve one man for the fower daies exercise of trayning, and a nomber which, by reason of the churlishnes of their peeces and not being made acquainted therewith by degrees, are ever after so discoraged as eyther they winck or pull their head from the peece, wherby they take no perfect levell, but shoote at random and so never prove good shott.

[fo. 51b] An order for the trayning of shott without anie wast or great expence of powder.

[In another hand:] For Mr. Vicechamberlen, with the letter to him.

41. [fo. 45a]   Directions for Corporals. [1585?][1]

[Enclosed with No. 37]

[fo. 50b] Directions for Corporals. [In another hand:] For Mr. Vicechamberlen with the letter to him.[2]

42. [fo. 39a] [Letter. Hatton to Knightley and Montagu. 19 April, 1587.][3]

After my very hartie commendacions. Vppon the receipte of your last letters, advertizing the dishabilitie of the Shiere to furnishe the number of twelve hundred men with armour according to the prop[orcion] sett

[1] See **11** for another copy.
[2] These endorsements are in the same hands as those on **40**.
[3] The right hand edge of this letter has been worn away. Missing parts of words have been supplied in square brackets.

downe, I haue declared vnto my Lordes what stoare of armo[ur] the same maye conveniently yelde, who, vppon my perswasion, th[ey] ar pleased I sholde signifie unto you that for this firste yeare [you(?)] sholde leavie and putt in readines the number of six hundred foote onely, according to the rate of your furniture, and one hundred horse. Wherein you ar to haue especiall care that the same number maye be very well chosen and appoincted, bothe for their aptenes and hable[nes] of bodie (as men selected to serve for the garde of her Majesties per[son]) and also for the furniture of their armour and weapons, the same be suche as maye in everie respecte be very serviceable, and them to haue in a readines vppon anie sodaine occasion that maye be offred for their employment.

According to which number I haue sett downe the names of suche gentlemen of the Shiere as, in my opinion, ar fitt to haue the leading of them, as shall appeere vnto you by the note here enclosed, subscribed with my hande; referr[ing] nevertheles the same to your discrecions, to be altered as you shall cawse, being better acquainted then my selfe with the state of the Shiere, the disposicion of the gentlemen, bothe for healthe [and] otherwyse, and anie other thing fitt to be considered herein. Wh[erein] I knowe you will haue due regarde that everie thing be perform[ed] in the best sorte for the advauncement of this present service.

And bicawse I vnderstand the Hundred of Nassaburghe, the Borrowe Stoke [sic] of Peterborowghe, hathe aunciently heretofore made their musters severally within them selves by auncient priviledge of that Hundred, I thincke it fitt these sholde be still continued entier vnto them, that they be not strayned to appeare at the generall place of your musters, s[o] the service be otherwyse sufficiently performed by them accord[ing] to the Lordes direccion. And this the rather in respecte of my very good Lorde, the Lord Treasurer, vnto whome the iurisdiccion of that Libertie dothe appertaine, and who (I am assured) w[ill] haue all honourable regarde for the due execucion of anie se[rvice] to be performed for her Majestie there.

And so prayeng your wonted good care and diligence in the accomplishement of the premisses, I bidde you very hartiely fare well. From the Cowrte at Grenewiche, the xixth of Aprill, 1587.

Your very loving assured frende,

"Chr: Hatton"

Sir Richard Knightley and Sir Edward Mountague

[fo. 42b] To my very worshipfull frendes, Sir Richarde Knightley and Sir Edwarde Mountague, knightes, Deputed Lieutenauntes of the Countie of Northampton.

[Armorial seal under paper]

43. [*fo.* 40a] [HATTON'S LIST OF FIT GENTLEMEN TO LEAD THE HORSE AND FOOT. 19 April, 1587.][1]

[*Enclosed with No. 42*]

MR. EDWARDE GRIFFIN, MR. EDWARDE SAUNDERS. To the leading of the hundred horse, viz: either of them fiftie.

MR. CHITTWODDE, MR. THOMAS BURNABIE, MR. ROGER KNOLLIS. To the leading of iij[C] footemen on the west syde.

MR. EDWARDE MOUNTAGUE, MR. WILLIAM BROWNE, MR. GILBERT PICKERING. To leade the other iij[C] footemen on the easte syde.

"CHR: HATTON"

44. [*fo.* 64a] [LETTER. HATTON TO KNIGHTLEY AND MONTAGU. 11 June, 1587. (*Copy*)][2]

After my [very[i]] harty commendacions. It hathe pleased her Majestie to wright her gracious letter vnto me with order to gyve direccion vnto you, the Deputed Leifetenauntes of the Countye of Northampton, for the levyinge of CC men to be presently imployed in her Highnes service in the Low Countryes vnder the charge of my very good Lord, the Earle of Lecester, her Majesties Lifetenant [Generall[i]] ther, to which purpos my Lordes of the Counsaile have likewise directed their letters vnto me, signifyinge her Majesties further pleasure in what sorte that nomber is to be levyed and with [what[i]] ease of charge to the Contrye, for the better and speidyer accomplishment therof.

And because by the same letters, which herewith I send you, you shall particulerly vnderstand the wholl course of that direccion, it shall not be neidefull for me to make any further repeticione therof by theis my letters, but onely earnestly to praye you that, in asmuche as her Majesties princelye goodnes appearethe towardes vs in not over charging the Contrye at this tyme with the wholl furniture requisite for that nomber, you will have an earnest care in [the[d] your[i]] choyce to be made of hable and very serviceable men in everye respect, the service intended beinge of soe great importance as it is.

So as it may appeare we have had an especiall regard of our duetyes in this behalfe, and that we maye [not[d]] be found nothinge inferyor to any other County in the settinge forthe of the nomber appoynted, bothe for the reputacione of our Countrye and her Majesties good opinione to be conceaved of vs, whom this charge have [*sic*] byne cheifly recommended vnto. Requiringe moreover that, accordinge to thefect of the letter here encloased[3] written vnto me by the said Lieutenant Generall, the said leavye maye be made with all convenyent expedicione, and the charge therof to be delivered over to this gentleman, Mr. George Nowell, expresly sent downe by his Lordship to receave the same of you.

In the performance of all which, not doutinge of your best cares and

[1] Summarised in *M.B.S.*, p. 9.
[2] At the top left hand corner of this page is written "ii" (for "11").
[3] Not extant,

endevours bothe for your owne credyt and myne, for the which I shall have greate cause to thanke you, I byd you hartely farewell. From the Courte at Greinewiche, the xjth of June, 1587.

CHR: HATTON, Chanc.

Sir Richard Knightley
Sir Edward Mountagu

[*At foot of this page:*] To the Right Worshipfull my very good frends, Sir Richard Knightley and Sir Edward Mountagu, knightes, her Majesties Deputed Lifetenantes in the Countye of Northampton.

45. [*fo.* 63a]   [LETTER. THE COUNCIL TO HATTON. 8 June, 1587.][1]

[*Copy. Enclosed with No. 44*]

After our right harty commendacions to your Lordship. Whereas the Queens Majestie hath occasion at this present to send over certaine forces into the partes of beyond the seaes [*sic*] for hir service and defence of the Vnited Provinces of the Low Cuntryes, vnder the chardge of our very good L[ord], the Earle of Lecestre, hir Highnes Leivetenaunt Generall in those partes, as will more particulerly appeare by hir Majesties owne letters at this present addressed vnto your Lordship; for as muche as hir Majestie, of hir accustomed goodnes, haveing consideracion of the present dearthe and other chardges that the sondry Countryes of this Realme have byn of late subiect vnto, ys loath emoungste the reste to burthen that County otherwise then of necessitye she is constrained, hir pleasure therefore ys that, by the Deputy Leivtenantes, the Countyes wher theis leavyes are appointed to be made shall be let vnderstand that hir meaninge ys not that, in the leuyeing and furnishinge of the number specified in hir Highnes said letter, the Countye should for the present be at anie furder chardge then to allow ten shillinges for every souldiour towardes the provision of a sword and dagger for him, and for conduct money, being carefull for the present to ease them of all suche other chardges, as of armour and coate money, as hath byn heretofore accustomed.

Wherefore seinge hir Majestie ys contented to deale thus favorably with the said Countye, and rather to supply the other wantes out of hir owne coffers then to overchardge hir subiectes, it ys expected that they should be the more willinge and carefull in the choyce of the men, to see them able and meet for service. And in this choyce we are to let your Lordship vnderstand that it ys not thought convenient that anie of them which were heretofore trayned should be imployed for this service.[2]

And whereas by your Lordships order the Deputy Leivetenantes shall

---

[1] At the top left hand corner of this page is written "io", (for "10").
[2] At this date the trained bands were normally reserved for home defence. See Cruickshank, p. 26.

have made choyce of the said nomber, hir Majesties pleasure ys that your Lordship or your Deputyes should cause a veiwe to be made of them before suche capten as the said Earle of Lecester shall send downe in to that Countey to receive them, to thintent he maye have the likeing [and^d] or refusinge of the persones, so as the bandes maye be well furnished, wherevpon he ys allso appointed to receive them at the said Deputye Leivetenantes handes, with that rate of money only as ys before expressed, to thintente they maye be by him conducted to the sea syde, to be from thence transported over according to suche direccion as the said capten shall receive from the said Earle.

And so prayeing your Lordship to have a speciall care hereof, so as the service maye be duely done and that no default maye be found in yow or your Deputyes to the contrary, we bidd your Lordship right hartely farewell. From Gree[n]wich, the eight of June, 1587.

Your Lordships very loveing freindes,

W: BURGHLEY   C. HOWARD   F. KNOWLYS   J. CROFTE
F. WALLSINGHAM   J. WOLLEY

To our very good Lord, the Lord Highe Chauncellor of Englond, hir Majesties Leivetenant in the Countie of Northampton.

46. [fo. 78a] [LETTER. HATTON TO KNIGHTLEY AND MONTAGU. 11 October, 1587.]

After my very hartie commendacions. By order from her Majestie it hathe pleased my Lordes of the Counsell to directe their letters vnto me for the putting in readines the forces of that Shiere (as her Majesties Lieutenaunte Generall there) with all convenient speede, vppon speciall consideracions moving her Highnes thereunto. The which letters I haue thowghte fitt to sende herewith vnto you as her Majesties Deputed Lieutenauntes for thexecucion of those services, to thende you maye proceede with expedicion to thaccomplishement of theffecte of those letters, according to their Lordshippes precise direccion therein contayned, aswell for the viewing and mustering, furnishing owte the iuste number of your said forces bothe on horse and foote, and performing of all other [thinges^i] necessarie in suche good sorte as the importaunce of the service shall requier. Wherein as I assure my selfe of your wonted good care and earnest endevours, according to the speciall trust reposed in you among others, in a matter of that waighte and momente, so muste I still remember vnto you that my chief desier is that in theise preparacions our Countrie may be founde inferiour to none of the rest in a cawse tending as greatly to her Majesties service and satisfaccion and the generall safetie of the Realme, whereof I know you will haue all due care and regarde.

And of your proceedinges herein, desiering to be particularly certified in wryting, to thende I maye emparte the same to her Majestie according to the direccion of the aforesaid letters, I bidde you bothe moste hartiely fare well. From London, the xjth of October, 1587.

Your very lovinge assured frende,

" CHR :   HATTON,   Canc. "

Sir Richard Knightley
Sir Edward Mountague

[*fo.* 81b] To the Right Worshipfull my very good frendes, Sir Richarde Knightley and Sir Edwarde Mountague, knightes, her Majesties Deputed Lieutenauntes of the Countie of Northampton, and to either of them.

[*Further endorsement in Montagu's hand:*] The lettere I rec[eived] of Worteley the messenger, the xiij^t of October, about iiij in the afternone.
[*Traces of seal*]

47. [*fo.* 77a] [LETTER. THE COUNCIL TO HATTON. 9 October, 1587.][1]

[*Enclosed with No. 46*]

After our verie hartie commendacions to your Lordship, the Queenes Majestie being sundry waies at this present informed of the great preparacions now presentlie made readie in Spayne for the furniture of a might[y] armie with a nauie to come speedelie to the seas, and having gre[ate] cause to doubt of some attempt therbie to be made against some parte of her dominions, hathe thowght it most necessarie that her whol[e] Realme should forthwith be well garded and in readines with suche strength as God hath geven her Majestie both by land and sea. And therefore amongest other meanes which her Majestie mindeth to vse by having an armie vppon the seas, her pleasure is that you, having charge as her Majesties Lieutenant Generall over that Countie of Northampton, should be heerof aduertised, and that you showld presentlie without any delaie vse all good and speedie meanes first to conside[r] of such former instructions and directions as yow haue receaved fo[r] the putting of the forces vnder your charge in strength, and thervp[on] to cause all persons heertofore mustred to be in redines with thei[re] armour and weapons, so as they maye with their captens and leaders vppon all suddain warning or occasion speedelie repaire to suche places as by former instructions they ought to be. And if anie be dead or departid out of the Countie, to appoint new sufficient persons in their places.

And though yow shall not haue conuenie[nt] time to make anie generall musters, yet you shall doe well in eue[ry] quarter of the Shire

---
[1] The edge of this letter is badly rubbed and parts of words have been conjecturally supplied. The letter is summarised in *M.B.S.*, p. 18.

to cause a view to be made in all the hundr[eds] by such as, where your selfe cannot be personallie, the same maie be dulie performed by men of credit and vnderstanding. Because hir Majestie would be satisfied what accompt she maie make of the numbe[r] and the forces of her subiectes, as well horsmen as footemen, in all places, and of all their captaines and leaders, her expres comma[nd] is that you shall forthwith and without delaie certefie in writing the nombers of all sortes that are furnished and be able to serue, and who are their captaines and petie captens, making in your certificat the distinction of their weipouns.

And for this seruice her Majestie willeth that no delaie of time be vsed herein, but that all the forces vnder your c[h]arge maie be made readie to march with all their furnit[ure] vppon an howres warning to such places as occasion shall require to withstand all manner [of] attemptes by anie enimie.

Wherof her Majestie being aduertised from yow in what sorte yow shall proceed and what number you shall haue in readines, she shall conceaue such coumfort as by Gods grace her Realme and her good subiectes shall, notwithstanding the great forces of her ennemies, be able to repulse and make frustrat[e] the same, to the honnor of her self and of her Realme.

And so not doubting of your Lordships great care in the performance of the premisses according to the trust reposed in you, we bid your Lordship right hartelie farewell. From the Court at Richemond, the ixth of October, 1587.

Your Lordships verie assured loving frends,

"CHR: HATTON, Canc." "W. BURGHLEY" "H. DERBY"
"C. HOWARD" "F. KNOLLYS" "FRA: WALSYNGHAM" "J. WOLLEY"

[*At foot of fo. 77a on the left:*] Lord Chancelor
[*At foot of fo. 77b on the right:*] A. Ashely

[*fo. 82b*] To our verie good Lorde, the Lorde Chancelor, her Majesties Lieutenant Generall ouer the Countye of Northampton.
[*Further endorsement:*] X 1587, October 9. My Lordes of the Counsell.
[*Yet another endorsement in another hand:*] That your Lordship as her Majesties Lieutenaunt in the Countie of Northampton doe give order that the forces of that Shiere may be in readines for her Majesties service vppon presente warninge.

[*Traces of seal*]

48. [*fo.* 85a] [A RATE FOR KEEPING HORSES. 18 October, 1587.][1]

Decimo octouo [*sic*] die Octobris 1587

A rate for keping of horses in the West Parte of the
Cownty of Northampton:

		Demilances	Light Horses
	Henry Lord Compton	[blank]	[blank]
	John Wake	[blank]	1
ded	Thomas Catesby	[blank]	1
	Sir John Spencer	1	2
	Thomas Morgan	1	1
dead	Thomas Andrewe	1	1
	Euseby Isham	1	1
ded	Francis Worly	[blank]	1
	Sir George Farmor	1	2
	Thomas Furthoe	[blank]	1
	Thomas Cave	1	[blank]
	William Sanders	[blank]	1
	Richard Burnabey	[blank]	1
	John Read	[blank]	1
	Mistris Shugborowe	[blank]	1
	Georg Sherly	I	2
Ireland	William Clarke	[blank]	1
	Thomas Kirton	[blank]	1
	Foulke Odull	[blank]	1
	Samwell Danvers	[blank]	1
	Crescent Butry	[blank]	1
	Richard Foxe	[blank]	1
	John Blincowe	[blank]	1
	[William Dormor*d*]		1
	Richard Chitwood	1	1
	Thomas Emely	[blank]	1
	Jerom Farmor	[blank]	1
	Francis Barnard	[blank]	1
	Augustine Crispe	[blank]	1
	Tobias Chauncey	1	[blank]
	Albon Butlor	[blank]	1
ded	Robert Pargiter	[blank]	1
	Roberte Wasington [*sic*]	[blank]	1
	Edward Cope	1	[blank]
	Erasmus Dreidon	[blank]	1
dead	Thomas Harby	[blank]	1
	Francis Foxley	[blank]	1
	William Hicklinge	[blank]	1
	[Roberte Harboro*d*]		1
	[Moris Miles*d*]		1
+	John Freman	[blank]	1
	William Samwell	[blank]	1
	Summa	10	Summa 40 [*sic*]

[1] This is an amended version of the list in *M.B.S.*, p. 19; see above, p. xx. The marginal
notes were evidently made at a later date, since Thomas Andrew did not die until 1594.

	Demilaunces					Light Horses
Sir William Hatton, knight .	1	.	.	.	.	2
Sir Richard Knightley . .	1	.	.	.	.	[blank]
Michaell Stuttesburie [and] Jeames Kenricke . . .	[blank]	.	.	.	.	1
Lawrence Manley . . .	[blank]	.	.	.	.	1
John Britten [and] Edward Knight	[blank]	.	.	.	.	1
John Neale	[blank]	.	.	.	.	1
John Brian [and] John Kirtland	[blank]	.	.	.	.	1
Gifford Watkin [and] [blank] Creswell	[blank]	.	.	.	.	1
Roberte Hartwell . . .	[blank]	.	.	.	.	1
Edward Onlie	[blank]	.	.	.	.	1
Anthonye Stratford [and] George Dredon . . .	[blank]	.	.	.	.	1
Amye Braie vidua . . .	[blank]	.	.	.	.	1
Anthonie Morgan [and] Love of Aynoe	[blank]	.	.	.	.	1
William Wattes [and] Firmyn Russell	[blank]	.	.	.	.	1

49. [*fo.* 84a] [LETTER. THE EARL OF LEICESTER TO THE JUSTICES OF THE PEACE. 31 January, 1587/8. (*Copy*)]

After my verye hartye commendacions. The Queens most excellent Majestie having a [s. .ᵈ] especial care of [*sic*] her good and loving subiectes shall not be greved, iniured and wronged by the leude dealing of any her ministers and now namely purveighors, who of long time haue (as is supposed) vnder pretence of her Majesties Commission abused this office contrary to the lawes of this Realme in the case provided. And for as much as yt hath pleased her Majestie to call me to the place of Lord Steward within her most honorable house, and to giue speciall charge as a principall officer vnto whom the reformacion of such abuses doth chiefly apertaine to haue care hereof, I am therefore hartely to pray you, and euery of you, that at youre next assembly and meting together you make diligent search and inquiry aswell of all discordes and misdeymanours comitted by anie purveor or carior of Commission for anie provicion for the service of her Majesties house, as also what somes of mony any person or persons can cleme by bill taile or debentur for any provicions whatsoeuer, from the xvᵗ yeare of her most gracious raigne vntill this presente tyme, but most especially for this iiij yeares last past; to thende that not onely seueritye and punishment may be vsed vppon offendors to the good example of others, but also that all persons hauing specialtes as aforesaid to make demaund for mony duely for provicions so taken and not paid for, may make there repaire or trew certificat before me and other the officers of the Greencloth, where the matter shalbe duely examined to the better ssatisfacion of [othersᵈ] all those vnto whom

any such somes of monye shall apeare to be due. And for that the
disorder of purveiors hath ben long complened of, and that 1 wish
them rather extinct for the ease of the countrye then with seuerıtye
still to punish such offendours as are rooted in an euill custome of
misdemeanore, as her Majestie herselfe of her most gracious inclinacion
towarde all her loving subiectes is desirous to ease them of those takers
and purveiors if her house might otherwise be provided for, as for my
part through youre industry and care I thinke it may be, so will I also
adde my best indevour hereunto, if that some two or three of you doe
repaire before mee and the rest of the Greene Cloth, to offer such
reasonable service vnto her Majestie (by way of compoticion) |sic| of
such previcions as youre country doth best yeeld; wher I doubt not
but, vppon such conference as we shall haue together, we shall grow to
some such good agreement as shall tende aswell to the great quietnes
of her subiectes as to her owne more agreeable service, with youres
and mine owne also very great contentacion.

Thus preing you to haue speciall care of the premisses and to vse
what expedicion conveniently may be therein, I bid you hartly farewell.
From the Court, this last of January, 1587.

Youre very loving freende,
R. LEYCESTER

50. [fo. 79a] |LETTER. HATTON TO KNIGHTLEY AND MONTAGU.
(6?) February, 1587/8.][1]

After my very hartie comendacions. Whereas lately it pleased of the
Councell for certaine speciall respectes to directe their honourable letters
vnto me, towching the restraincte of suche recusantes of that Countie
as in theise daungerous tymes mighte be th[ought] moste fitt to be delt
withall, forasmuche as I nowe vndersta[nd] by you, Sir Richarde Knightley,
that vppon the viewe of those letters addressed vnto me you haue
hitherto forborne to [accom]plishe theffecte of their Lordshippes direccion
therein, attending su[che] particular order from me in that behalfe, I haue
therefore thowghte good for your speedie proceeding in that service [to]
requier you vppon the receipte hereof to enter into the due consi[deracion]
and execucion of their Lordshippes said direccion, according to those
le[tters] which I sende you here enclosed, and to performe the contents
th[ereof] in such sorte as maye be aunswerable to their expectac[ions]
and the truste by me committed vnto you for thexecucion of anie h[er]
Majesties services in that Countie.

Wherein not dowbting [you] will vse that care and diligence that shall
be fitt, I bidd [you] very hartiely fare well. From London, the vj [?]
of Februarie, 1587.

Your very loving frende,

" CHR: HATTON, Canc. "

[1] The right hand margin of this page has been cut or rubbed off. Missing parts of
words have been conjecturally supplied in square brackets.

Sir Richard Knightley and Sir Edward Mountague, Deputie Lieutenantes of Northampton Shiere.

[*fo.* 80b] To the Right Worshipfull my very good frendes, Sir Richarde Knightley and Sir Edwarde Mountague, knightes, her Majesties Deputie Lieutenauntes of the Countie of Northampton, and to either of them, give theise.

[*Part of armorial seal under paper*]

51. [*fo.* 83a]   [LETTER. THE COUNCIL TO HATTON. 4 January, 1587/8.][1]

After our right hartie comendacions vnto your good Lordship. Wheras her Majestie haue thou[ght] it most conuenient, beinge aduertised sundry wayes of the great preparacions tha[t] are mad a broade of shippinge and men, to prouide all things necessary to defende any invacion or attempt that might be made against the Realme or other her Highnes dominions, emongest other thinges consideringe howe of lat years diuers of her subiectes by the meanes of badd instrumentes haue ben with drawen from the dewe obedience they owe to her Majestie and her lawes, in so much as diuers of them most obstinatly haue refused to come to the Church to prayer and deuine seruice; for [asmu^d] which respectes, beinge so addicted, it is hardly ventured to repose that trust in them which is to be looked for in her other good subiectes, and it is also certaine that such as should meane to invade the Realme woulde neuer attempt the same but vppon hope which the fugatiues and rebells ofer to giue and assure them of those badd members that all ready are knowen to be recusauntes, it is therefore thought meete in these doubtfull times they shoulde be so looked vnto and restrained as they shall neyther be able to giue assistaunce to the enymie, nor that the enimy may haue any h[ope] of releife and succour by them.

Wherefore her Majesties pleasur is, your L[ordship] shall cause dewe enquire to be made what nomber of recusauntes are in that Countie and of what quallitie and abillitie they be of, wherin such gentlmen as haue ben Comissioneres [before^i] in those matters are able to instruct you, and there vppon to cause the most obstinat and noted persons to be comitted to such prisons as are fittest for their saffe keepi[ng]; the rest that are of valur and not so obstinat to be referred to the c[usto]die of some eclesiasticall persons and other gentlmen well affected to remaine at the charges of the recusant, to be restrained in such sort as they may be forthcominge and kept from intelligence the on of the other.

Wherin hopinge your Lordship will take such order herin as shalbe most requisit in that behalfe, we bid your Lordship hartely farewell. From the Court, the 4th of [December^d] [January^i], 1587.

Postscript. We praie you also to advertise vs of the names of those

---

[1] The edge of this letter has been badly rubbed and parts of words have been conjecturally supplied.

recusantes you shall comitt, either to prisons or to the custodie of others, and how thei are bestowed.

Your very louinge freindes,

"W. BURGHLEY" "H. DERBY" "JO. CANT." "CHR: HATTON, Canc."
"C. HOWARD" "F. KNOLLYS" "JAMYS CROFT" "A. POULET"
"T. HENEAGE" "J. WOLLEY"

[*At foot of page, on left:*] Lord Chauncellor

[*fo.* 88b] To our verie good Lord, the Lorde Chauncellor of England, Leivetenaunte Generall of her Majesties Countie of Northampton.

[*Further endorsement:*] This lettere was delyvered to T(?) Mychell, measenger, the xxijth of January at my howse at Barnewell, saing he hadd noe other letter from my Lord Chauncellor.[1]

[*At foot of page:*] Northampton

[*Remains of seal of Privy Council under paper*]

52. [*fo.* 91a] [LETTER. HATTON TO SIR THOMAS CECIL, KNIGHTLEY AND MONTAGU. 5 April, 1588.]

After my verie hartie commendacions. I sende you here enclosed two severall letters directed vnto me by her Majesties commaundement, whose pleasure is to be presently certified of the forces of that Countie (as of all other Shieres of the Realme besydes) bothe of horse and men, and all other necessarie furniture thereunto belonging.

Theise shall be therefore to requier you that vppon the receipte hereof you doe presently enter into that busines according to the direccion of their Lordships letters, and that vppon a full viewe had of your forces and furniture (as is aforesaid), you doe forthewithe certifie the same in wryting vnto me, observing the order of the certificate here enclosed, whereby everie thing required maye the more playnely and distinctly appeere, remembring lykewyse vnto you that everie other Shiere, bothe for horse and men, furniture of armour, weapon, shotte and all other necessaries, ar fully provided according to the aforesaid note, as appeerethe by their particular certificates allready sent vpp vnto my Lordes.

Wherein I feare we shall be founde sumwhat behynde the rest, a thing especially to be looked vnto, bothe in the respecte of our diuties as also for the reputacion of our Countrie and our owne particular affeccions to shewe our forwardnes in her Majesties service, in which I wolde be loathe we sholde be founde (for the number) inferiour to anie other Shiere, so far forthe as the habilitie of our Countrie maye afforde it. The rather for that it is ment that of the 600 rated vppon our Shiere, 400 ar to be sent vp hither to ioyne with other forces according to the descripcion of an armie of 4,000 appoincted to remayne here, to be employed as cawse of

---

[1] This endorsement does not seem to be in Montagu's hand.

service shall requier. [*Inserted here in the margin in the same hand as the text:*] which purpose you maye not publishe, but retaine and keepe vnto your selves vntill you here further from me.

My earnest desier, therefore, is that your choice bothe of horse, men and furniture maye be founde to be suche as maye in everie respecte aunswer her Majesties expectacion, and that in anie wyse your captaines (or their lieutenauntes at the leaste) may be appointed men sufficient and experte in service and fitt to take the charge of suche bandes which by your good endeavoures I truste shall be provyded for accordingly. And evenso, I bidde you bothe [*sic*] very hartiely fare welle. From the Courte at Grenewiche, the vth of Aprill, 1588.

Your very loving frende,

" CHR : HATTON, Canc. "

[*fo.* 91b] *Postscript.* The Commission of my Lieutenancie[1] beinge renewed unto me for certain imperfeccions in the former Commission, as uppon the viewe thereof shall appeere unto you, I haue lykewyse sent you herewith the Commission it selfe for the more expedicion, prayenge you forthwith to cawse a copie thereof to be taken for your owne vses, and with all conuenient speede [to returne[1]] the same unto me, for my warrante as in that case it behouethe, &c.

Sir Tho: Cecill
Sir Rich: Knightley and
Sir Edw: Mountague

[*fo.* 92b] To the Right Worshipfull my very good frendes, Sir Thomas Cecill, Sir Richarde Knightley and Sir Edwarde Mountague, knightes, her Majesties Deputie Lieutenauntes of the Countie of Northampton, and to everie of them, give theise.

[*Traces of seal*]

[*Note. The above postscript is not in Hatton's hand.*]

53. [*fo.* 89a]   [THE COUNCIL TO HATTON. 2 April, 1588.][2]

[*Enclosed with No. 52*]

After our right hartie comendacions to your Lordship. Wheras the Queenes Majestie is dalie geven to vnderstande of the continuance of the great preparacions of the Kinge of Spaine, which are thought to be intended towardes these partes, her Highnes, beinge desirous to vnderstande the generall estate of the forces of the whole Realme, hath caused such certificates to be viewed as hath ben sent hither from suche as

---

[1] No copy of this is extant. For the circumstances of its issue, see above, p. xxiii.
[2] Summarised in *M.B.S.*, p. 19.

hath ben heretofore appointed Lieuetenauntes in sondrie counties of this Realme.

And forasmuch as, contrarie vnto her Majesties [and[d]] and our expectacion, it is found that no suche certificates [as[i]] hath ben sent vpp from your Lordship, her pleasure and comaundement hath ben that we should signifie so much vnto your Lordship and earnestlie to require your Lordship forthwith, with all the speede that possiblie maye be, to cause a view of all the horsemen and trayned men of the counties vnder your Lordships Lieutenaunce to be made, so as the bandes maye be complete and seuerally trayned with as much ease of the Countrie as maye be, in convenient nomber accordinge to former directions, so as the same maye be in a readines to be employed as occacion shall require.

And to thintent the saide certificates maie be made in due order accordinge to her Majesties desire, and in such forme as others haue don, we haue thought good to sende vnto your Lordship hereinclosed, a patern in what sorte the same should be made, which we praye your Lordship to retorne vnto vs accordingly, with all the speede that possiblie maye be.

And so bidd your Lordship right hartelie farewell. From Grenwich, the second of April, 1588.

Your Lordships verye lovinge frendes,

"W. BURGHLEY" "R. LEYCESTER" "C. HOWARD" "T. HENEAGE"
"FRA: WALSYNGHAM" "J. WOLLEY"

Northampton

[fo. 94b] To our verie good Lord, Sir Christopher Hatton, knighte, Lord Chauncellor of England, and her Majesties Lieutenaunte for the Countie of Northampton.

[Further endorsements:] 1588. Aprill 2. My Lordes of the Councell.

That your Lordship give order the [certifi[d]] number of horsemen and trayned soldiours in the Countie of Northampton be certified vpp to their Lordships according to the forme of the certificate here enclosed.
Northampton.

[Traces of seal]

54. [fo. 90a] [LETTER. SIR FRANCIS WALSINGHAM TO HATTON. 2 April, 1588.]

[Enclosed with No. 52]

My very good Lord,
Her Majestie hath geven me express commaundement to send vnto your Lordship and also all other Lieutennantes of other Counties to knowe what martiall men you haue within the Countie vnder your Lieutenancy who haue served in the warres as capteines, lieutenantes,

ensignes or corporalls. And theerfore I am to praye your Lordship to direct your letters to the capteines aswell of the trayned bandes as of others, requiring them to make a perticuler certificat of the names of the sayd martiall menn and of the charges which they haue borne and howe they ar nowe ymployd in any of the bandes vnder your charge; and herin to vse all expedition possible for that her Majesties purpose is that yf the Counties shall not be sufficiently furnished of such persons able to take charge of the bandes, that then some meanes shalbe thought vppon to se them furnished by some other waye.

And so not doubting of your Lordships care and diligence in this behalf, as the necessitie of the present time doth requier, I take my leaue. From the Court, the 2 of Aprill, 1588.

Your Lordships to commaunde,

"FRA: WALSINGHAM"

[fo. 93b] To the righte honorable Sir Christopher Hatton, knight, Lord Chancellor of England and Lord Leivetenante of the Countie of Northampton.

[Further endorsements:] [1] 1588. Aprill 2. [2] Mr. Secretarie Walsingham. [3] That letters may be directed by your Lordship to the captaynes of trayned bandes and others to sende vpp a particular certificate of the names of all [the*] martiall men within the Countie of Northampton. This to be done by commandment of her Majestie.

[Armorial seal under paper]

55. [fo. 95a] [LETTER. HATTON TO SIR THOMAS CECIL, KNIGHTLEY AND MONTAGU. 13 April, 1588.]

After my very hartie commendacions. I haue receaved your aunswer to the late dispatche I sent vnto you for the mustering of the forces of that Shiere, and for a certificate thereof to be made to be sent vpp vnto my Lordes, wherein I perceave your readines and earnest care to accomplishe that service according to their Lordships dirreccions, for the which I hartily thancke you.

But forasmuche as I fynde you cannot proceede to thexecucion thereof, for that you want sufficient warrant of deputacion vppon this second Commission from which you ar to receaue aucthoritie as Deputie Lieutenauntes of the Shiere, I haue therefore sent you the said deputacion vnder . my hande and seale, together with the transumpte of the said Commission subscribed lykewyse by me, thincking it needles the same sholde otherwyse be published by proclamacion, seing it contayneth no alteracion in substaunce from the former Commission, prayeing you vppon the receipte of the premisses to proceede with all expedicion to the accomplishement of the said service, and to advaunce the same by all the best meanes you can, which by your good endevours I trust shall

be performed accordingly, and therein I referre you to the aforesaid
direccions.

I haue appoincted Mr. Willm. Lane to receave the charge of horsemen
of my cosin Saunders, who hathe lykewyse order to deliver the same
over vnto him. And thus ending, I bidd you very hartiely fare well.
From London, the xiijth of April, 1588.

Your very loving frende,

"CHR: HATTON, Canc."

Sir Tho. Cecill
Sir Rich. Knightley
Sir Edw. Mountague

[fo. 100b] To the Right Worshipfull my very good frendes, Sir
Thomas Cecill, Sir Richarde Knightley, and Sir Edwarde
Mountague, knightes, her Majesties Deputie Lieutenauntes of the
Countie of Northampton, and to everie of them.

56. [fo. 97a] [LETTER. HATTON TO CECIL, KNIGHTLEY AND
MONTAGU. 15 June, 1588.][1]

After my very hartie commendacions. I haue receaved letters from
my Lordes of the Councell towching summe preasent service to be
performed with all convenient expedicion, the which letters I sende you
here enclosed, earnestly requiring you to see the contentes thereof duely
executed so far forthe as shall appertaine. And bicawse it is lykewyse
resolved by my Lordes that 400 of the number of men charged vppon
that Countie shall be sent vpp to attende here at the Cowrte, and to be
ioyned with greater forces for the defence of her Majesties person, it shall
be very needefull you haue especiall regarde the said number be well
and choycely furnished in everie respecte, very well provided of good
and experte captaines fitt for the lyke charge, and to be in readines
vppon the firste warning, whensoeuer they shall be commaunded to
repaire hither for that purpose. Wherein it behoveth vs to be the more
carefull, in respecte of the greate favour vowchesafed vnto vs by her
Majestie in charging our Countrie with so small a number, where everie
other Shiere of the Realme is to supplie allmoste thrice the dubble of
that number.

The conduccion hither of the 400 men so to be sent vpp is thowghte
fitt to be committed vnto Sir Richarde Knightley, as one of the Deputie
Lieutenauntes, and a gentleman very meete to be employed in the accion
of that service, namely, to see them orderly browghte vpp and delivered
here, and [they[i]] then to be disposed as by their Lordshippes shall be
thowghte convenient, and your selfe to followe suche further direccion
as it shall please them to appoincte you vnto.

The Provoste Marshall mencioned in their Lordshippes letter wolde,
in my opinion, be summe experte gentleman inhabitaunt in that

1 This letter is summarised in *M.B.S.*, p. 20.

Countrie, wherein I desire to be advertized from you whom you shall fynde aptest for that purpose.

And thus referring the accomplishement of theise thinges delivered in speciall charge vnto me to your wyse and [cha^d] carefull regarde, I bidde you all very hartiely fare well. From the Courte at Grenewiche, the xvth of June, 1588.

Your very loving assured frende,

" CHR: HATTON, Canc. "

Sir Tho: Cecill
Sir Rich: Knightley
Sir Edw. Mountague

[*fo.* 98b] To the Right Worshipfull my very good frendes, Sir Thomas Cecill, Sir Richarde Knightley, and Sir Edwarde Mountague, knightes, and to everie of them, give these with speede.

[*Traces of Seal*]

57. [*fo.* 96a] [LETTER. THE COUNCIL TO HATTON. 15 June, 1588.][1]

[Enclosed with No. 56]

After our right hartie commendacions to your good Lordship. The Queenes Majestie beinge certanly [adver]tysed that the Kinge of Spaynes Navye is already abroade on the seas and gon to [the] coaste of Byscay, whereby yt is to be doubted the same maie take some course to m[ake] some attempte on suche parte of the Realme as shalbe thought fytt for his purpose, [where]of as yet we cannot knowe anie certenty, for which respecte her Majestie hath tho[ught] yt convenient your Lordship should be advertysed thereof to thende you maie geve presente ord[er] to all the gentlemen that are captaines and leaders of men in that County in noe wyse [to be] absent out of the Shire; and to haue especiall care that the nombers of the sev[erall] bandes be full and complete, to which end notyze shalbe geven and straight co[mman]dement to all the souldiers of the trayned bandes in lyke manner to remain[e] in the countrey and in noe wyse to be out of the waye, that vppon an howers [war]ninge they maye be in a readines to be imployed as occacion shall serve, vppon payne to be commytted to pryson for the spayce of fortye dayes and further puni[shment] at the discrecion of your Lordship and your Deputie Lieutenauntes; of which bandes yt is tho[ught] expedient that there shoulde be a presente viewe taken, that they and theire furniture maie be certenly seene to be complete and thoroughly furnished.

---

[1] The edge of the right hand margin of this letter has been rubbed off. Words and parts of incomplete words have been conjecturally supplied in square brackets. This letter is summarised in *M.B.S.*, p. 20.

[We] are lykewyse to praie your Lordship that the lyke care be had to see the beacons [wat]ched in suche sorte as hath ben appointed, and those other ordres put in execucion and duely observed with all speede and dilligence which haue ben sett down [and] devysed for the better defence of the Realme, and for preparinge and puttin[ge] in a readines with convenient speede the forces of the said County.

And bec[ause] in such doubtfull tymes yt falleth out commonly that dyvers false rumours and rep[ortes] are geven furthe and spreade abroade, which doe dystracte the myndes of the people and breed confusion, yt is thought verie requisyte a care should be had hereof, and that the authours of suche rumors and tales should be dilligently fo[und] out from tyme to tyme and severely and speedely punished. For better execuc[ion] wherof, because there are verie manie vagrante and idle persones that goe about [the] countrey fitt to be evill instrumentes in all bad accions, it is alsoe thought v[erie] requisyte at this presente for the chastesinge of suche lewde persons and prevent[ing] those inconveniences that by them maie anie way aryse, that you shall appo[int] a Prouost Marshall accordinge to the auctority geven your Lordship by your Com[mission] of Lieutenauncy, to pervse[1] the Countrey and to be assysted in all places by Jus[tices] and constables, for the apprehension, stockinge and imprisoninge of them, y[f] they will not geve them selves to labor.

Wherein prayinge your Lordship that spe[ciall] dyreccion be geven in this behalfe, for at this present noe delayes nor anie slacknes ys to be vsed, we byd your Lordship verye hartely farewell. From the Courte at Grenewych, the 15th of June, 1588.

Your Lordships assured lovinge frend[es],

" W. Burghley " " R. Leycester "
" H. Hunsdon " " F. Knollys " " T. Heneage "
" Fra: Walsyngham " " Wa: Mildmaye " " J. Wolley "

Lord Chauncellor

[fo. 99b] To our very good Lord, Sir Xpofer Hatton, Knight, Lord Chancellor of Englande, and her Majesties Lieutenante in the Countie of Northampton.

[Seal of the Privy Council under paper]

58. [fo. 101a] [LETTER. HATTON TO CECIL, KNIGHTLEY AND MONTAGU. 22 June, 1588.]

After my very hartie commendacions. Whereas it hathe pleased her Majestie to directe her gracious letters vnto me towching summe extraordinarie proporcion of furniture to be presently supplied, aswell in that Countie as ellswhere, among the better and wealthier sorte towarde the defence of her Highnes person and Realme in this daungerous and suspicious tyme of invasion, I haue thowghte good, respecting the weight and importaunce of the service nowe to be

---

[1] To travel through scrutinizingly.

performed, to sende vnto you the originall letter it selfe,[1] to thende you maye the better vnderstande thereby her full meaning and intencion, and therevppon proceede to the due execucion of her will and pleasure with all thexpedicion that the said service shall requier; which chiefly consistethe in this, that everie man acc[or]ding to his habilitie and degree doe forthewith putt him selfe into furniture in summe larger proporcion then hathe ben certified heretofore, especially at this instant, wherein everie of vs is to thincke aswell vppon the preasent defence of our private and particular estates, as of the generall cawse it selfe, for the which theise preparacions wer first ment and appoincted.

I sende you lykewyse herewith a letter written vnto me by Mr. Secretarie Wallsingham,[2] by which (as you shall perceave) he callethe vppon me for a particular certificate of the forces of that Countie according to the forme prescribed and sent vnto you heretofore, which I assure you hathe ben looked for long since and thowghte sumwhat straunge it hathe not ben hitherto receaved. I praye you lett it be presently performed with the residue contayned in the said letter, to thende that we among others be not noted to make defaulte in so necessarie a service as this.

And where you desier to receave summe newe direccion from me towching the further trayning of your forces, as a thing very chargeable to the Countrie, as therein I dowbte not but you haue taken especiall care to see them kepte in suche exercise as they maye be founde very sufficient to serve when tyme shall requier, so must you in anie wyse holde on that course still (thowghe to summe further charge vppon so waightie a respecte as dothe enforce it), to thende that the number to be sent vpp proove, neither for skill or otherwyse, inferiour to the trayned companies of anie other Shiere.

Whereof assuring my selfe you will haue that necessarie care and regarde (bothe for your owne reputacion and myne) that in this case shall be fitt, I bidde you very hartiely fare well. From London, the xxij[th] of June, 1588.

Your very loving assured frende,

"CHR: HATTON, Canc."

Postscript. Bicause I knowe not in what sorte your soldiours haue ben hitherto trayned, I must in anye wyse requier you to see them trayned in suche good sorte and with suche speede as they may not be founde unequall with other trayned soldiours, as the necessitie of this seruice dothe requier, &c.

Sir Rich: Knightley
Sir Edw: Mountague

[fo. 106b] To the Right Worshipfull my very good frendes, Sir Thomas Cecill, Sir Richarde Knightley and Sir Edwarde Mountague, knightes, give theise with speede.

[Traces of seal]

[1] The Queen's letter, however, is not in this collection of papers.
[2] **59**.

59. [*fo.* 102a]   [LETTER. SIR FRANCIS WALSINGHAM TO HATTON. 19 June, 1588.]

[Enclosed with No. 58]

My very good Lord,
I haue thought good to put your Lordship in mynde to send away the certificate of the musters in the Countyes of Northampton and Middlesex vnder your Lordships charge according to the forme sent vnto your Lordship in Aprill last, to thend hir Majesty may be made acquainted with the state of hir forces in the said Countyes.[1] And also that it may please your Lordship to cause a certificate to be made of the martiall men resident in the said Countyes who haue serued in forrain partes according to my other letters written to your Lordship at the same tyme[2] by hir Majesties commaundement.
And so I humbly take my leaue. From the Court at Grenwich, the xixth of June, 1588.
Your Lordships to commaund,

"FRA: WALSYNGHAM"

Lord Chauncellor
[*fo.* 105b] To the Right Honorable my very good Lord, the Lord Chauncellor of England.

[Further endorsement:] 1588. June 19. Mr. Secretarie Walsingham. To putt your Lordship in mynde to send awaye the certificate of musters in the Counties of Northampton and Middlesex, and to cawse a certificate to be made of the martiall men resident in the said Counties, who haue served in foraine partes, etc.
[Seal, imperfect]

60. [*fo.* 103a]   [LETTER. HATTON TO CECIL, KNIGHTLEY AND MONTAGU. 18 July, 1588.]

After my very hartie commendacions. I am commaunded from her Majestie to signifie unto you that presently vppon the receipte hereof you sholde furnishe the number of fower hundred men (to be specially chosen owte of the forces of that Countie), with coates and conduicte money, to thende they may be in readines vppon the firste warning to be sent vpp to attende her Highnes person according to her former direccion; the color of which coates is referred to your discrecions to be suche as your selves shall thincke fittest for that purpose. But in any wyse you are to haue regarde to selecte the most apte and hable bodies for that service, and suche as you shall knowe to be well and diutifully affected in everie respecte as appertaynethe.

[1] See **53**.
[2] **54**.

It is veryely thowghte they shall be appoincted to marche on hitherwardes sumtyme the next weeke. I praye you therefore lett everie thing be in good readines as [shall^d] shall be fitt. Towching the charge of their coates and conduicte money, it is reason the Countrie it selfe sholde beare the same as other Shieres of the Realme ar to doe in the lyke case. The residue I referre to your good consideracions. And evenso I bidde you very hartiely fare well. From the Courte at Richemonde, the xviijth of Julie, 1588.

Your very loving assured frende,

"CHR: HATTON, Canc."

Sir Tho: Cecill
Sir Richard Knightley
Sir Edw. Mountague

[*Postscript, in Hatton's hand:*] My Lordes doo thynke it moste fitt that the whole number of 600 be sent vpp; which I pray you maye be thought of, notwithstange [*sic*] I will my best endeuoyer that the 400 may content them, &c.

[*Traces of seal*]

[*fo.* 104b] To the Right Worshipfull my very good frendes, Sir Thomas Cecill, Sir Richarde Knightley and Sir E. Mountague, knightes, and to everie of them, give theise with speede.

61. [*fo.* 107a] [LETTER. HATTON TO CECIL, KNIGHTLEY AND MONTAGU. 19 July, 1588.][1]

After my very hartie commendacions. Whereas by order from her Majestie the whole force of that Countie bothe of horse and foote ar forthwith to be putt in a readines to marche on hitherwardes vppon present warning, to be attendaunt abowte her Highnes person [or otherwyse employed as cawse of necessarie defence shall requier^r], and for that purpose ar to be provyded of all necessarie furniture accordingly, theise shall be to requier yow vppon the receipte hereof to take present order in that behalfe, by leavieing vppon the said Countie bothe coate and conduicte money, the charge whereof is to be borne by the Countrie it selfe as in lyke case hathe allwaye been accustomed heretofore. Which contribucion (I dowbte not) they [will^r] moste willingly yelde vnto, the waightines of the service considered, and the speciall favour shewed vnto them, above anie other Shiere of the Realme, the meanest of them being farre more overcharged bothe in expence and in number of men then owres, as I dowbte not is well knowen vnto yourselves and also to the whole Countrie.

I praye you therefor, lett this direccion be presently performed so as everie thing may be in a readines as appertaynethe, for the which theise shall be your sufficient warrant and discharge. And evenso I bidde yow

[1] Summarised in *M.B.S.*, p. 20.

very hartiely fare well. From the Cowrte at Richemonde, the xixth of Julie, 1588.

Your very loving assured frende,
" CHR : HATTON, Canc. "

Sir Thomas Cecill
Sir Rich: Knightley
Sir Edw: Mountague

[*fo.* 112b] To the Right Worshipfull my very good frendes, Sir Thomas Cecill, Sir Richarde Knightley, and Sir Edwarde Mountague, knightes, her Majesties Deputy Lieutenantes of the Countie of Northampton and to everie of them, give theise with speede.

[*Traces of seal*]

62. [*fo.* 108a] [LETTER. HATTON TO CECIL, KNIGHTLEY AND MONTAGU. 19 July, 1588.]

After my very hartie commendacions. Yesterdaye by direccion from her Majestie I wrotte vnto you, signifieng her pleasure that the 400 men which ar to attende her Highnes person here, [or for other employment as cawse of necessarie defence shall requier*] sholde be in a readines vppon preasant warning thereof to be given vnto yow. Since which tyme it hathe ben resolved by my Lordes in Councell (by lyke direccion from her Majestie) that the whole forces of that Countie bothe of horse and footemen sholde be called vpp and furnished for that purpose accordingly. I praye yow lett present order be taken for it, and see them in a readines to marche on hitherwardes abowte thende of nexte weeke at the fardest, for so it standes resolved as yett, wherof neverthelesse yow ar to receave particuler notice by speciall letters from their Lordshippes.

Towching the charge of coate and conduicte money, sythe all the other Shieres of the Realme ar to beare the same (as in lyke case hathe ben allwayes accustomed heretofore), and that our Shiere hathe ben specially favoured among the rest, bothe in expence and number of men, I hope they will not thincke it muche to yelde to this contribucion, especially in a service of this waighte and importaunce, and this the rather throwghe your good perswasions, as also for that, so soone as they shall be delivered here into her Majesties armie, that charge shall cease and they ar presently [to] be eased thereof.

Mr. Griffin hathe ben lately discharged and is nowe at libertie.[1] Order shall be therfor given vnto him from me for the provision of suche furniture as hathe ben charged vppon him, and that with all convenient expedicion, to thende he maye ioyne the same with the rest.

As for my cosin Saunders, he bearing nowe thoffice of Highe Sheriffe and having by that meanes POSSE COMITATUS at his direccion, it

[1] In April, 1588 Griffin and Saunders had incurred the privy council's displeasure for their failure to settle a dispute over property: *A.P.C.*, xv, 20.

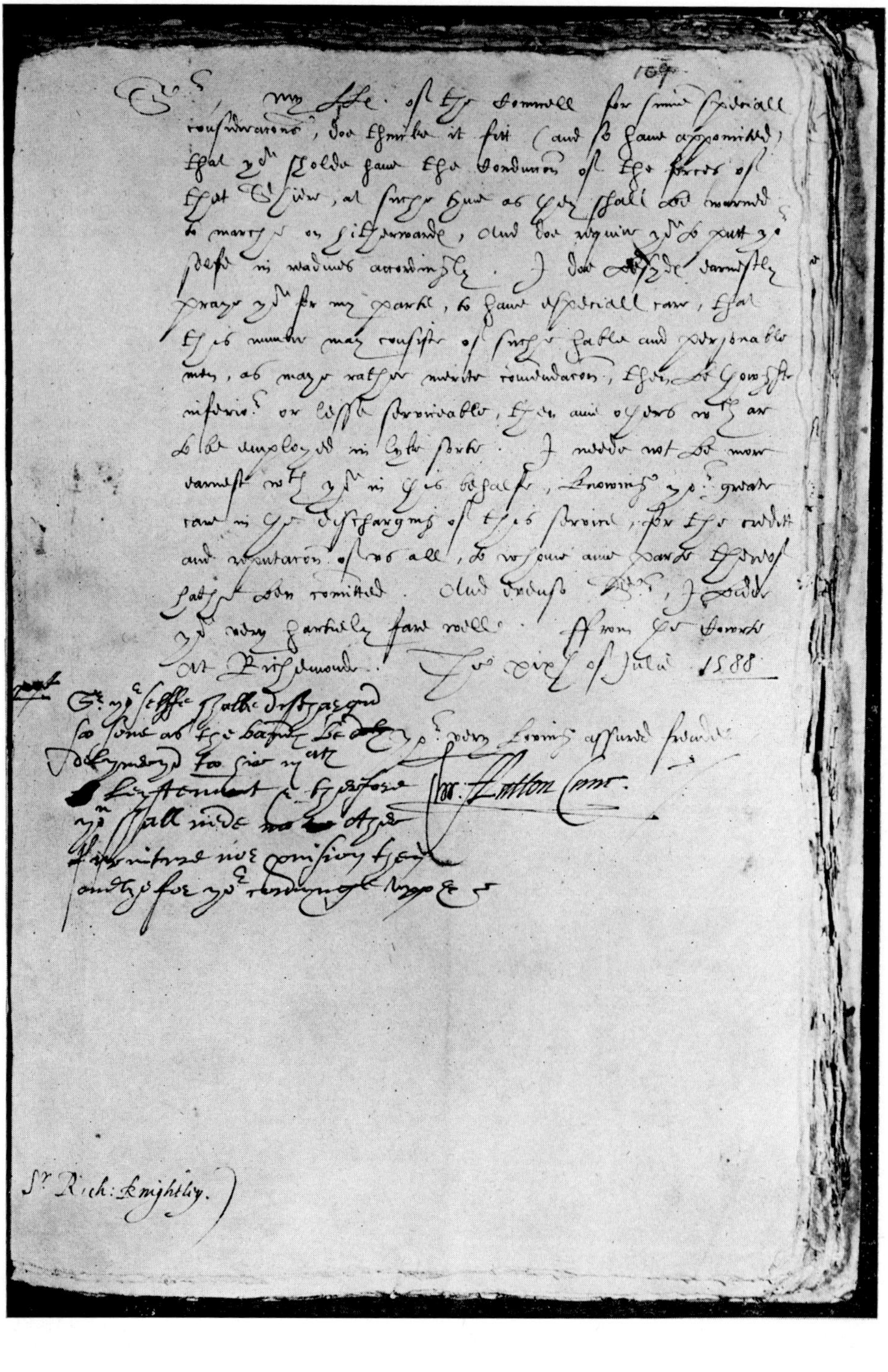

107

Sr, my LLs. of the Councell for some speciall consideracons, doe thinke it fitt (and so have appointed) that you should have the conduction of the forces of that Shire, as such tyme as they shall bee warned to marche or sett forwarde, And doe require you to putt your self in readines accordinglie. I doe also earnestlie pray you for my parte, to have speciall care, that this number may consiste of such hable and personable men, as maye rather merite commendacon, then be thought inferior or lesse serviceable, then anie others wch are there employed in like sorte. I neede not bee more earnest wth you in this behalfe, knowinge your greate care in the discharginge of this service, for the creditt and reputacon of vs all, to whome anie parte thereof hath bene comitted. And thus Sr, I bidd you very hartelie fare well. ffrom the Courte at Richmond. The xixth of Julie 1588.

Sr, my selfe shalbe discharged so sone as the bande be delyvered to [illegible] lieutenant [illegible] therefore you shall neede [illegible] [illegible] [illegible] for your [illegible] &c.

Your very lovinge assured frende
Chr. Hatton Canc.

Sr Rich: Knightly.

LETTER FROM HATTON TO KNIGHTLEY (No. 63)

were no reason his horses sholde be taken from him for the tyme being to be employed ellswhere.

My chief care is that everie thing be duely and orderly performed in the furnishing owte of theise forces, agreable to her Majesties expectacion, wherein assuring my selfe of your best endevoures I bidde yow very hartiely fare well. From the Courte at Richemonde, the xixth of Julie, 1588.

Your very loving assured frende,

" CHR : HATTON, Canc. "

Postscript.

I haue receaued the certificate from you, the order whereof is very well lyked and allowed of here, and my Lords doe yelde you their very hartie thanckes for your paynes and travell in that behalfe.

[*fo.* 111b] To the Right Worshipful my very good frendes, Sir Thomas Cecell, Sir Richarde Knightley, and Sir Edwarde Mountague, knightes, and to everie of them, give theise.

[Traces of seal]

63. [*fo.* 109a]   [LETTER. HATTON TO KNIGHTLEY. 19 July, 1588.]

Sir,

My Lordes of the Councell for summe speciall consideracions doe thincke it fitt (and so haue appoincted) that yow sholde haue the conduccion of the forces of that Shiere at suche tyme as they shall be warned to marche on hitherwardes, and doe requier you to putt your selfe in readines accordingly.

I doe besydes earnestly praye yow for my parte to haue especiall care that this number may consiste of suche hable and personable men as maye rather merite commendacion then be thowghte inferior or lesse serviceable then anie others which ar to be employed in lyke sorte.

I neede not be more earnest with you in this behalfe, knowing your greate care in the discharging of this service, for the creditt and reputacion of vs all to whome anie parte thereof hathe ben committed. And evenso, Sir, I bidde yow very hartiely fare well. From the Cowrte at Richemonde, the xixth of Julie, 1588.

Your very loving assured frende.

" CHR : HATTON, Canc. "

Post[script].[1]

Sir, your selffe shalbe discharged soo sone as the bandes be delyueryd too hir Majesties Leyftennant, and therfore you shall nede no other furniture nor prouision then onelye for your comynge vpp, etc.

[1] This postscript is in Hatton's hand.

Sir Rich: Knightley

[*fo.* 110b] To the Right Worshipfull my very good frende, Sir Richarde Knightley, knighte, one of her Majesties Deputie Lieutenauntes of the Countie of Northampton, give theise.

[*Traces of seal*].

64. [*fo.* 118a]　[LETTER. HATTON (TO KNIGHTLEY AND MONTAGU?) 23 July, 1588. (*Copy*)][1]

After my hartie commendacions. I send you thencloased directed vnto me from my Lordes, prayinge you not to fayle in any wise to accomplishe with all care and diligence as well this as all other ther and my former direccions in that behalfe. And wher you have earnestlye moved me for some respecte to be had in the easinge of the charge of the Countye, I must lykewise herin require you to consyder the wayght and necessetye of this [cause[d]] service, thenymyes attempt beinge more playnlye discovered, his forces aryved vppone the coast of the one [syde[d]] part, and other forces likewise in readynes to be landed from hower to hower by the Duke of Parma, to the common daunger of the Realme and cheiflye of her Majesties most reall persone.

I praye you therfore vse all necessarye perswasyones in this case. Noe other Shire of the Realme be nighe soe well and favorablye delt with all as ours, I cann assure you. The ressydue I referr to your good discressiones. And even soe I byd you verye hartelye farwell. From the Courte at Gremwich [*sic*], the xxiijth of July, 1588.

Your verye lovinge assured frend,

" CHR: HATTON, Canc. "

65. [*fo.* 113a]　[LETTER. THE COUNCIL TO HATTON. 23 July, 1588.] (*Copy*)][2]

After our hartie commendacions to your good Lordship. Wheras vppone the discoverye of the repayre of the Spanyshe armye vppone the coast of this Realme yt is thought meite and convenyent that a suffycient nomber of horsse shuld presentlye repayr to the Courte to attend one her Majesties persone, theis are therfore to signyfie vnto your Lordship that her Highnes pleasure is that you shall, with all convenyent speid that maye be vsed, send hether suche nomber of launces and lyght horsse as was contayned in your last certyficate [to be (?)] sent hether vnder the conduct of those gentlemen to whom the leadinge of the said horsses was commytted.

---

[1] This and **66** are copied on to the second sheet of the copy of the Privy Council's letter to Hatton of 23 July, 1588 (**65**).
[2] Summarised in *M.B.S.*, p. 20.

Prayinge your Lordship herin not to fayle to gyve order that they maye be here by the fourthe of this next monethe, we byd your Lordship hartelye farewell. From the Courte at Richmonde, the 23 of July, 1588.

Your Lordships very lovinge frendes,

CHR: HATTON, Canc.   WILLM. BURGLEY   FRANCIS KNOWLES
THO: HENAGE   FR: WALLSINGHAM   J. WOLLEY

Postscript.

Furthermore vppon further resolucione her Majesties pleasure is that you shall send from thence the nomber of 600 footmen to be led by their captaynes and offycers to Londone by the xxixth of this mounthe, and that some specyall persone maye have the generall charge to conduct them thether.

66. [*fo.* 118b] [LETTER. HATTON (TO KNIGHTLEY?) 28 July, 1588. (*Copy*)]

Sir,

My Lordes, for the better service of her Majestie in this daungerous tyme, have thought yt verye requisyde that a colleccione of archars should be made in everie shire of the Realme, and for that purpose have commaunded that I, by vertewe of my offyce, should gyve order that enquirie be made in that our Countye what nomber of men the same myghte convenyentlye furnishe out with that kynde of weapon. I praye you therfore presentlye vppone the receipt herof to make pryvate inquirie therof in the Shire, whether the same myght amount to the nomber of 200 good and hable bowemen. And alsoe to wyshe shuch [*sic*] as you shall fynd apt for that kynd of service to be in readynes with ther furniture, to be imployed as further occazione shall require.

Herin for the present you shall neid to proceide noe further then this vnlesse you shall receave particuler direccione from my Lordes, to see them mustered and conveyed to any other place wher in you are with all care and diligence to accomplishe ther Lordshippes order. The performinge wherof referred to your wonted good discrecione, I byd you right hartelye farewell. From the Courte at Richmond, the xxviijth of July, 1588.

Your verye lovinge assured frende,

CHR: HATTON, Canc.

Postscript.

I praye you, Sir, certyfie me your oppynione soe soone as convenientlie you maye, what you thinke maye be doone herin, &c.

67. [*fo.* 114a]   [LETTER. HATTON TO KNIGHTLEY. 29 July, 1588.]

Sir Richarde Knightley,

Whereas I have receaved your letters of the xxviijth of this present monethe in the which you desire to have some direccion where you shall bestow your men when they are comen vpp to London, I have thought good to signefye vnto you that I holde it fitt you should, with all the speede you maye, repaire hether vnto London, and there you can not want lodginge nor places for the bestowing of them. Yf there fall out any accident wherebye you may stande in neede of vsinge my helpe in this behalf, I will be readie to vse all good meanes I maye [to my Lord Generall *interlined in a different hand*] for your ease and relief therein.

And so wishing you [not*d*] to vse all the diligence you may [soe you brynge your forces together *interlined in a different hand*] for your speedye repaire hether, in as muche as the tyme requirethe no lesse, I commende you to the good keeping of Almyghtie God. From Eely Place, the xxixth of Julye, 1588.

Your assured loving frende,

"CHR: HATTON, Canc."

Sir Richard Knightley

[*fo.* 117b] To the Right Worshipfull my very lovinge frende, Sir Richarde Knightley, knight, geve these.

68. [*fo.* 124a]   [LETTER. MONTAGU TO KNIGHTLEY. 30 July, 1588.][1]

After my verie hartie commendacions. I have sent you herinclosed a note of the chardges and allowances of Captayne Browne and Captayne Nicolls, together with a callender of all the soldiers. Thus praying God to preserve her Majestie, send peace to the Realme, and to you a prospeorovs jorney with health, I leave you to God. Northampton, this xxxth of July.

Your asswered frend,

"E. MOUNTAGU"

[*Traces of seal*]

[*fo.* 119b] To the Right Worshipfull and my verye good frend, Sir Rich: Knightlye, knight, theis be delivered.

---

[1] This letter is written on the back of Captain Browne's and Captain Nicolls' Accounts (**69**), which Montagu was sending to Sir Richard with the lists of the soldiers for the east division (**70** and **71**).

69. [*fo.* 119a]   [CAPTAIN BROWNE'S AND CAPTAIN NICOLLS'
ACCOUNTS FOR THE EAST DIVISION. 30 July, 1588. (*Enclosed
with No. 68*)][1]

Paide vnto Captaine Browne for his allowaunce, the xxxth daie of
July, 1588, at Northampton, as followeth:-

Firste for one hundreid and fiftie coates at fifteene shillinges a coate	j^cxij *li.* x*s.*
For conduct money for one hundreid and fiftie men at ten shillinges a man	lxxv *li.*
Item allowed and payde to the captaine for the leadinge of them	xx *li.*
Item paide more unto him for the repaireinge and tryminge of his armour, shott and weapon . .	x *li.*
Item geiven to his leivetenant Mr. Bartholomew Morgan in reward	ls.
Item paide more vnto the captaine for ten holberdes	iij *li.*
Item geiven more to his seargantes, drume and corporalles	v *li.*

Summa totalis: ij^cxxviij *li.*

"WYLLYA' " BROWN[2]

Paide vnto Captaine Nicholes for his allowaunce the xxxth daie of
July 1588 at Northampton, as followeth:-

Firste for one hundreid and fiftie coates at fiftene shillinges a coate	cxij *li.* x*s*
For conduct money for one hundreid and fiftie men at ten shillinges a man	lxxv *li.*
Item allowed and payde to the captaine for the leadeinge of them	xx *li.*
Item paide more vnto him for the repayreinge and tryminge of his armor, shot and weapon . .	x *li.*
Item geiven to his leivetenant Mr. John Goodfelloe in rewarde	ls.
Item geiven more to his seargantes, drumne and corporalles	v *li.*

Summa totalis: ij^cxxv *li.*

"FRAUNCIS NICOLLS"

Summa totalis: ccccliij *li.*

[1] Printed in *M.B.S.*, pp. 20-21.
[2] Browne apparently gave up the struggle after writing "Wyllya", and "Brown" is in
the clerk's hand.

70. [*fo.* 158a] The Names of suche Soldyers as are vnder the Leadinge of Captaine Browne. [30 July, 1588].[1]

[Enclosed with No. 68. This list is in columns in the original]

[*Column 1.*] Tho. Johnsone, Willm. Dillingham, Tobye Selbye, Peter Fysher, Ro: Ryppone [*for* Ryxxone?][2], Ro: Androwe, J. Hullocke, Geo: Fisher, Rich. Myles, Ja: Chambers, Henry Warren, J. Knight, Henrye Frisbie, Ja. Gilpine, Tho. Rippone, Tho. Loftis, Ric. Basse, Rowland Grosse, Nicholas Doltone, Humfrye Head, Nicho. Peter, Tho. Dobbes, J. Wilbore, Ro. Wyse, Jeffery Marckam, Ro. Welbie, W. Coles, Edw. Peake, Henrie Willimot, William Welles, Gregorie Car, J. Danford, Tho. Prydmore, Humfrye Frysbie, Tho. Allen, Tho. Hawlie, J. Collyer, Arthur Chambers, Rich. Broughtone, Geo. Selbie, Edmonde Jhonsone, Roger Slawsone, Edw. Frauncis, Rich. Bosworthe, W. Newbone, Henrie Howe, Tho. Judd, Tho. Darlinge, Tho. Bull. W. Templer, Ro. Clynche, Rich. Templer, W. Taylbie, Jhon Hunt, Jhon Jhonsone, Willm. Sechell, R. Powell.

[*Column 2.*] Tho. Phippes, Nichol. Addams, W. Smythe, Henrie Dexter, Gilbert Iuxone, Rich. Sprigge, Jefferie Collyer, W. Palmer, Symon Davye, Kellam Conygrave, Rich. Gill, W. Butler, W. Brigg, Tho. Chambers, Jhon Lye, Jhon Latham, W. Boman, Geo. Whitte, J. Pickeringe, J. Eston, Phillipp Hensone, Geo. Jenkes, J. Pen, Nicho. Smythe, Rich. Phuncocke, Tho. Head, W. Bull, W. Hunt, Tho. Lussell, W. Baylie, Tho. Selbye, Tho. Tomlynsone, Lawrance Myles, Willm. Younge, Rich. Mosbye, Tho. Smythe, Tho. Beningtone, Tho. Goodman, Mathew Wright, Mychaell Bunch, Tho. Stanyerne,

THE SOAKE OF PETERBRUGHE
Ro. Stringer, Tho. Wood, W. Jerman, Ro. Wilbore, J. Lamkine, Ro. Whitte, J. Byrd, W. Coxe, Tho. Darbie, Wolfred Darbye, J. Torner, Geo. Clarke, J. Barnwell.

[*Column 3.*] Jho. Butcher, Henry Ham, Ro. Clem't [*for* Clement?], Allen Bell, Tho. Byrd, Adam Robynsone, Tho. Mortymer, Charles Smythe, J. Smythe, Rich. Addysone, Edw. Wilbore, Rich. Dawsone, Ro. Barker, Francis Dredwaye, Henry Sawford, W. Warrine, J. Lott, Randole Styles, Tho. Clarke, Tho. Orginer, W. Strettone, Gowm [*sic*] Arnestead, J. Ferman, J. Fletcher, Xpofer Addysone, Athanasyus Charington, J. Berslye, Lawrance Warrest, Tho. Eckles, Willm. Lanketone, Nathanyell Basset, Ro. Everie, Tho. Covell, W. Linsleye.

---

[1] See *M.B.S.*, p. 21, where part of this list is printed.
[2] See *ibid.*, where this name is " Ryxone " which, as Rixon, is still a local name in Northamptonshire.

71. [*fo.* 159a] THE NAMES OF THE SOLDYERS VNDER THE
LEADINGE OF CAPTAINE NICCOLLES. [30 July, 1588.]

[*Enclosed with No. 68*]

[*Column 1.*] Rich. Drawater, Henry Drewerie, Charles Larratt, Jho.
Symond, W. Hunt, Humfrye Tebbott, Wolston Baxter, J. Peacham,
J. Sheltone, Ro. Symondes, Nicho. Dawes, J. Pyborne, Henry Vnderwood,
Henrie Packe, Henry Weckleye, W. Gates, Symond Tootyll, J. Wollastone,
Symon Bates, Geo. West, [Edw. Brookes*d*] Tho. Wallis, Ro. Wallis, Edw.
Smart, W. Tolyne, J. Pratt, Tho. Crosborowe, Edw. Hotone, W. Hobsone,
J. Baule, W. Bucke, W. Kent, W. Bawe, Peter Cleye, W. Wattell,
J. Richardsone, Tho. Baule, Rafe Spencer, Tho. Fysher, W. Browne,
Tho. Lane, Ro. Abbatt, Rich. Pratt, J. Allam', W. Hull, Henry
Curtice, W. Leye, Tho. Lickoras, Ro. Browne, Mark Gent, Gyles Curtice,
Steven Pumfrett, Tho. Bill, Tho. Harysone, Eusabie Goldsbie.

[*Column 2.*] Henrie Rowell, Tho. Burgis, Tho. Whitte, Tho. Sylbye,
Tho. Rogers, Tho. Blatt, Willm. Taylor, Nichol' Eastwicke, Tho. Hawlle,
Tho. Packe, Geo. Coledge, Tho. Hardwicke, J. Haryat, Danyell Powers,
Olyver Buckland, Steven Homes, W. Wimprose, J. Bletsoe, Geo. Osnam,
Nicho. Manninge, J. Page, Nicho. Masone, Ro. Hewett, Ja. Chapman,
Edm. Dykes, Tho. Fysher, Tho. Burgis, Henry Chapman, Mychaell
Heywood, Henrye Haule, Ro. Saundersone, Nicho. Mathewe, Tho.
Marchall, Willm. Clarke, W. Spencer, W. Cox, Rich. Chychile, Tho.
Eakyns, Xpofer Robynsone, J. Rowe, Geo. Boothe, Henry Dowse, J.
Maunsill, Basyll Sarjant, Rich. Heyre, Fr. Bull, Rich. Spellie, J. Allen,
Ro. Rowledge, Geo. Lychfeild, Rich. Eakins, Rich. Cable, Edw. Smythe,
Ryse Barrett, Tho. Clarke, J. Walter.

[*Column 3.*] Edw. Moorye, J. Bridgman, Edw. Seale, Edm. Eales,
Tho. Bent, Everett Boltone, Matthew Berne, Davye Hull, Frauncis
Hawford, Tho. Hull, Edw. Wade, Edw. Buswell, J. Clipsam, Edw. Wade,
sen', Frauncis Bosworthe, J. Paybodie, Tho. Dunmore, W. Taylour, Rich.
West, W. Whitwell, J. Abreye, J. Blasone, W. Engille, Tho. Mumford,
Owen Dawes, Rich. Skinner, Tho. Robbynsone, Edw. Brookes, Humfry
Prat.

72. [*fo.* 160b] [CAPTAIN KNOWLES' AND CAPTAIN BURNABY'S
ACCOUNTS FOR THE WEST DIVISION. 5 August, 1588.][1]

1588. The sums of money that have been collected within the West
Dyvicion of the Cownty of Northampton for coates and conducte, and
other necessaries for this her Majesties last service, the vth of August.

Sutton Hundred	.	.	.	.	lxv *li.* xvs.	
Norton Hundred	.	.	.	xxxij *li.* xs.	
Clely Hundred	.	.	.	.	xxxvij *li.*	ccxiij *li.* [*sic*]
Tocester Hundred	.	.	.	.	xxxviij *li.* xs.	
Wymersly Hundred	.	.	.	.	xlix *li.* vs.	

[1] Also in *M.B.S.*, pp. 21-23.

Faulesly Hundred	lxv *li*. x*s*.	
Wardon Hundred	xxxvij *li*. x*s*.	
Guilsborow Hundred	lx *li*.	ccl *li*.
Newbotle Hundred	liiij *li*.	
Spello Hundred	xxxiij *li*.	
Northampton Town	xxx *li*.	

[*Total:*] cccciiij^{xx} xiij *li*. [*i.e.* £493].[1]

Whereof paid to Capten Knowles at Islington about the vth of August, 1588, as followeth:

Item paid to him for cl cottes at xv*s* a coate, cxij*li*. x*s*.
Item paid to him for conduct money, of cl, at x*s* a man, lxxv*li*.
Item allowed him for leadinge of them, xx*li*.
Item more paid to him for dressinge his armour, x*li*.
Item gyven to his livetenant Moreton, l*s*.
Item more to his drumm, serient and corporalles, v*li*.
Item to the quarter master to provide ther loginges, vi*li*. xiij*s*. iiij*d*.
Item paid for iiij^{xx} poundes of powder to practise by the wey, the souldiers marchinge to London, v*li*. xiij*s*. iiij*d*.

Summa ccxxxvij*li* vj*s*. viiij*d*.

Paid to Capten Burnabey for his allowance in the same daie and yere as followethe:

Item paid to him for a cl coates at xv*s*. a coat, cxij*s*. [*sic*] x*s*.
Item for conducte money for cl men at x*s* a man, lxxv*li*.
Item allowed to the captaine for leadinge of them, xx*li*.
Item more to him for repairinge and bryninge[2] vp of his armor and weapon, x*li*.
Item gyven to his livetenant Courtney ... l*s*.
Item gyven more to the drumm, seriant and corporalls, . . v*li*.
Item paid to a carter for caringe of the horsmens armors, . . . xlij*s*.

Summa ccxxvij*li*. ij*s*.

The som of the paimentes to bothe captens and their companies in toto is iiij^C [lxviij*li*.^{*d*}] lxiiij*li*. viij*s*. viij*d*.

Thes is to be answered to the captens for the re car[i]ge of ther armor into the Contry.

SUCHE MONEY AS THE HIGHE CUNSTABLES OF EUERY HUNDRED PAID VNTO THE CAPTENS AND COMPANIES FOR TRAIN[IN]GE DAIES AS FOLLOWETHE:-

Item paid to Capten Knowels for traini[n]ge at Toceter, v daies, his own att v*li*. a daie, . . . xxv*li*.

---
[1] The correct total is £503.
[2] This may signify " bringing " or " burning " (for " burnishing ").

Item to his officers for the same v daies . . . iij*li*.

Item to the trained men [cl*ᵈ*] [iijC*ᵈ*] [cl*ⁱ*] for ther wages for the same v daies . . . xxv*li*.

Item paid for powder for the shott for the same daies v . . . xij*li*. x*s*.

Item paid by the highe cunstables for the cariedge to London of all our harmors for the iij*ᶜ* men, for vj cartes, xxviij*li*. viij*s*.

Summa iiij*ˣˣ* xiij*li*. xviij*s*.

Item to Captaine Burnabey for train[in]ge at Daventry, v daies, his allowance v*li*. a daie, . . . xxv*li*.

Item to his officers the v daies, xl*s*.

Item the trained men v daies at 8*d*. the daie, clxxv*li*. [*sic*]¹

Item paid for powder for the shott at 1*s*. a daie for the same v daies, xij*li*. x*s*.

Summa lxiiij*li*. x*s*.

The whole sum of all paimentes to the captens and the compa[nies] with traine daies and cariage: vj*ᶜ*xxij*li*. xvj*s*. viij*d*.

[*fo*. 161b, *in top left hand corner:*] Northampton shire. East [*sic*] Devicion, 1588.

73. [*fo*. 115a] [LETTER. LORD HUNSDON TO KNIGHTLEY AND MONTAGU. 14 August, 1588.]

After my hartie commendacions. Wheras I vnderstand by Capten Knollys that certayne parties heerevnder named, being prest to serve as soldiours vnder him, have refused to come vpp according to ther dutie, theis are to requyre and pray yow to call the sayd parties before yow and, yf yow fynd yt to be true, to send them vpp hether to me, to receve such punishment as ther contempt heerein deserveth.

Whereof expecting that yow should not fayle, I bid yow hartelie farewell. At the Court at St. James, this xiiijth of August, 1588.

Your loving frend,

"H. HUNSDON"

[*The names of the parties follow in column:*] COUNTY NORTHTON: Thomas Addyngton of Potterspury, Robert Wyllmore of Northampton, William Emmerson of Cosgraue, Arthur Leeson of Abthorpe.

Sir Richard Knightley
Sir Ed: Montigew

[*fo*. 116b] To my verie loving frendes, Sir Richard Knightlie and Sir Edwarde Montigew, two of the Deputie Leiutenantes of the Countie of Northampton.

[*Traces of seal*]

¹ The correct figure is £25.

74. [*fo.* 120a] [LETTER. LORD HUNSDON TO CECIL, KNIGHTLEY AND MONTAGU. 14 August, 1588.]

After my hartie commendacions. Wheras yt hath pleased her Majestie to dismisse the companies of footmen which came out of that Cowntie to returne homewardes with ther captaynes, theis are to requyre and pray yow to take such order at ther coming that ther armor, furniture and coates maye be kept in some convenient place neere vnto ther aboades, to be delivered to them agayne when neede shall requyre; and that the sayd number of soldiors may be in a readynes to repayre hether agayne when neede shall requyre vpon any sodayne warning, when yt shall please her Majestie to send downe direction for them.

Whereof praying you to have such care that her Majesties service be not hyndered by your defaultes, I bid yow hartelie farewell.

At the Court of Snt. James, this xiiijth of August, 1588.

Your verie loving frend,

" H. HUNSDON "

Deputy Leiutenantes of Northampton.

[*fo.* 123b] To my verie loving frendes, Sir Thomas Cicill, Sir Richard Knightlie, and Sir Edwarde Montigew, knightes, Deputie Leiutenantes of the Cowntie of Northampton.

75. [*fo.* 125a] [LETTER. HATTON TO CECIL, KNIGHTLEY AND MONTAGU. 29 August, 1588.]

After my very hartie commendacions. I sende you thenclosed, rec[ei]ved from my Lordes, contayning certaine particular direccions vnto me, wherein they requier expedicion to be vsed and summe speedie aunswer from me thereunto. After the pervsal whereof, theise shall be to praye and requier you to see the same very carefully executed in everie poincte, aswell in signifieng to our Countrie her Majesties gracious acceptacion and princelie thanckes for their readines and good willes shewed in this her late service, as also in returning speedie aunswer to suche particularities as their Lordshippes desier to be advertized of. Theffecting of all which I referre to your wonted good discrecions, bothe for the satisfaccion of my Lordes and the continuacion of their good opinion allready conceaved of vs, whereof I knowe you haue especiall regarde.

And evenso, I bidde you very hartiely fare well. From the Cowrte at St. James, the xxixth of Auguste, 1588.

Your very loving assured frende,

" CHR: HATTON, Canc. "

Sir Thomas Cecill
Sir Richard Knightley
Sir Edward Mountague

[*fo.* 130b] To our Right Worshipfull my very good frendes, Sir Thomas Cecill, Sir Richarde Knightley and Sir Edwarde Mountague, knightes, her Majesties Deputie Lieutenantes of the Countie of Northampton, and to everie of them, give theise.

[*Traces of seal*]

76. [*fo.* 121a] [LETTER. THE COUNCIL TO HATTON. 25 August, 1588.]

[Enclosed with No. 75]

After our hartie commendacions to your good Lordship. Her Majestie, vnderstandinge by late occacions of service the greate care your Lordship hathe had and the Deputie Lieutennantes within your charge haue taken in these publyke services committed to your charge, and speciallie in choyce of good and hable men, and prouidinge that they might be furnished with armour, weapon and other furniture, as appeared by those which were sent hither out of that Countie (wherof her Majesties self hathe ben an eye witnesse), doethe greatlie commend your Lordships care and diligence and travayle of your Deputie Lieutennantes, yieldinge to your Lordship and them her princelie thanckes in that behalf.

And wheras her Highnes is geven to vnderstand that there haue ben greater colleccions made in that Countie for armour, coates, conduct money and lyke furniture by the highe constables and other inferiur officers then hathe ben employed in the present service, her Majestie havinge a greate care to haue her good and lovinge subjectes well dealt withall; her pleasure is we should require your Lordship to geue order to your Deputie Lieutenauntes, callinge vnto them the Justices in the severall diuicions, to examine what summes of moneye at seuerall times haue ben gathered and collected of the Countrey and for what vses, to whose handes the same cam, and how the same hathe ben employed, to thend that it maye appeare to those that haue [collected*ᵈ*] [contributed*ᶠ*] so willinglie to these publyke services, to what vse the same was levyed and how employed. And if greater summes haue ben collected then haue ben bestowed for publyke service, that then restitucion maye be made. And where lykewise her Majestie hathe ben aduertised that certaine captens haue taken moneye of the trayned and appointed souldiors to dispence with them and take hierlinges in their places, if anie such abuse hathe ben committed in that Countie, we pray your Lordship the same maye be also examined and enformacion geuen to vs therof, that we maye cause those captens to be punished to the example of others, and satisfaccion made to the partyes whome they haue wronged.

Moreouer where there is a reporte geven forthe that that [*sic*] some of those souldiors which were at the Camp at Tilbury doe complaine that they haue not receyued their full paye for the tyme of their service there, for because the seuerall captens of the bandes haue receyued the whole enterteinment due to the souldiors from the time of their arriuall at the Campe vntill the dissolvinge of the same, who are charged to see the souldior satisfyed, and this reporte is a thinge very slaunderous to her Majestie; it is thought meete your Lordship should take notice therof to thende, if anie souldiors that were leuyed in that Countye be vnpaid of anie parte of their enterteinment, they maye by your Lordship be referred to the captens vnder whome they serued, to be aunswered at their handes, whome we doubt not if they were gent[lemen] of that Countye to haue that care of their reputacion as they will not with hold anye duetie from the souldior; wherin neuertheles, if anie defaulte should be found, you maye call them before you and cause them to see the souldior contented for that which is due to them, or otherwyse aduertyse vs of the [faulte^d] [same^f] if the capten were not chosen of that Countie, that we maye take order therin for the satisfaccion of the souldior.

We are further to require your Lordship that you will take some good order and care for those souldiors which were sent from thence, and are now retorned thither, that their armour, weapon and furniture maye be viewed and charge geuen vnto them to see the same were kept and preserued, according to the direction, as we doubt not but you have allreadie receaued from our very good Lord, the Lord Steward, that was Generall of the said armye in that behalf.

So we bid your Lordship right hartelie fare well. From the Courte at St. James, the xxvth of August, 1588.

Your Lordships verye lovinge frendes,

"CHR: HATTON, Canc." "W. BURGHLEY" "H. DERBY" "COBHAM" "F. KNOLLYS" "T. HENEAGE" "FRA: WALSYNGHAM" "A. POULET" "J. WOLLEY"

Wee requier you to vse somme speed for thexamynacion of the partes of all this letter, and therevpon to make answer so soone as you maye to every point thereof, for so the time requireth.

[*fo.* 122b] To our verie good Lorde, the Lorde Chancelor of England, her Majesties Lieutenant of the Countie of Northampton.

NORTHAMPTON

77. [*fo.* 126a] [LETTER. HATTON TO SIR WALTER MILDMAY. 4 October, 1588.]

Sir,

For aunswer of your late letter vnto me, it maye please you to vnderstande that I thincke it very requisite you sholde vowchesafe vs your wonted helpe and assistaunce in accepting the place of one of the Knightes for our Shiere againste this nexte Session of Parlamente. A trowble, I knowe, it will be vnto you, which you coulde be contented to avoyde, but seing it concernes the common cause[1] I truste you will the more willingly yelde vnto it, forgetting your owne quiett as in lyke case you haue ever done heretofore, for which the whole Shiere and my selfe

---

[1] A word has been struck out here and " cause " inserted above the line.

in particular shall rest muche beholding vnto you.

My good frende Sir Richarde Knightley offrethe to be lykewyse assistaunte vnto you in that service, and to supplie the place of the other Knighte for the Shiere, whome I thincke you shall fynde very plyable in anie thing you shall iudge convenient for the benefitt of our Countrie, wherevppon I doe lykewyse recommende him by my letters to the gentlemen my frendes there.

Thus, Sir, allwaye readie and bolde to trowble you, but with assuraunce of your good and frendlie acceptacion thereof, being yowres as I am with my best commendacions, I leave you to the Lorde Almightie. From London, the iiijth of October, 1588.

Your true frende very assured,

" CHR : HATTON, Canc. "

Sir Walter Mildmaye

[*fo.* 129b] To the Right Honourable Sir Walter Mildmaye, knighte, one of Her Majesties moste Honorable Privie Counsell.

[*Traces of seal*]

78. [*fo.* 127a]   [LETTER. HATTON TO KNIGHTLEY. 4 October, 1588.]

Sir,

I doe thincke it very fitt, according to my wonted good opinion allwayes helde of you, that your selfe sholde ioyne with my honourable good frende Sir Walter Mildmaye in executing the place of one of the Knightes for our Shiere in this nexte Session of Parlament. To which effecte I [am*d*] [doo*i*] preasently [to*d*] directe letters to the Sheriffe of the Shiere, and to other my good frendes there, that in this their eleccion they will be pleased to yelde you their voices and willing consentes in that behalfe, not dowbting but that throwghe your good endevour suche care shall be hadde for the weale and proffitt of our Countrie in everie respecte as shall be fitt and convenient.

And evenso, good Sir Richarde Knightley, prayeng you to holde this bearer your man excused, whom I cowlde not dispatche hence sooner by reason of my late phisicke, I bidde you very hartiely fare well. From London, the iiijth of October, 1588.

Your very loving assured frende,

" CHR : HATTON, Canc. "

Sir Richarde Knightley

[*fo.* 128b] To the Right Worshipfull my very good f·ende, Sir Richarde Knightley, knight, give theise.

[*Traces of seal*]

79. [*fo.* 131a] [LETTER. HATTON TO KNIGHTLEY AND MONTAGU. 23 January, 1588/9.]

After my very hartie commendacions. I haue receaved letters from my Lordes of her Majesties Councell concerning suche loanes of money as ar to be made vnto her Highnes in that Countie for a supplie of charge in her present affaires, greatly importing the whole state of the Realme, as is not vnknowen vnto you. For the better execucion whereof it hathe pleased their Lordshippes to sett downe very particuler instruccions as shall appeere vnto you by thenclosed[1], so as I neede not to make anie repeticion thereof by theise my letters, referring you wholy to thorder therein prescribed.

And for your further informacion of the cawse moving her Majestie to requier theise loanes at the handes of her subiectes, I haue lykewyse thowght good to sende you herewith their Lordshippes former letters written vnto me, which you maye vse according to your discrecions for the advancement of the service as you shall see cawse, bothe for the better satisfaccion of our Countrie as also to make the same the more willing to accomplishe this her Majesties request.

I earnestly praye you, bothe for your zeale and diutie to her Highnes and for your good frendshippe towardes my selfe, to proceede herein with all due care and diligence so as it maye take that successe which is expected, the rather throwghe your good travells and throwghe my earnest solicitacion vnto you in that behalfe. Wherein not dowbting of your wonted good endevoures shewed allwayes heretofore in all other occasions of her Majesties service, I bidd you very hartiely farewell.

From London. The xxiijth of Januarie, 1588.

Your very loving assured frende,

"CHR: HATTON, Canc."

Sir Richard Knightley
Sir Edward Mountague

[*fo.* 136b] To the Right Worshipfull my very good frendes, Sir Richarde Knightley and Sir Edwarde Mountague, knightes, and to either of them, give theise.

[*Traces of seal*]

80. [*fo.* 137a] [LETTER. MONTAGU TO KNIGHTLEY. 13 February, 1588/9.]

(Holograph)

After my verye hartie commendacions. I haue sente vnto you herewith

---

[1] The council's letters are not in this collection. Knightley, if he received them, may have passed them to Montagu, who had sole responsibility for the collection of the loan while his colleague was attending Parliament.

a letter vnto my verie good Lorde, the Lord Chancellor of Englande, towchinge the service of the Privie Seales which I praye you take soe much paines as see it delivered (requyring an answere) because of the truste that is reposed to you and mee in that service.

And forsomuch as theire be divers that finde them selves greeved with the charge thereof, bicause they are not of habilitie to lende any such somes as are demaunded of them, who woulde willingly do yt if yt were in them to performe the same, beinge much discontented to see that such as bee men of livinge and welthe are nothinge at all charged; therefore I have thought good to certefye you in a scedule hereinclosed[1] of the names of them with theire seuerall aunswers, and for your more redynes, although I knowe you can doe it better then I, if it please his Lordship to require any such thinge at youre handes, I haue sett downe the names of fortie persons out of which nomber supplie may be taken of the beste, meaninge that nether you nor I shoulde preferr any man, except it bee his Lordships pleasure to commaunde vs soe to certefy him, desyringe you to keepe the kalender of those names[2] newlie sett downe secretlie to your selfe; for I assure you I was never more trubled with any seruice in this County, hauinge such dailie suite for theire release, thinckinge that it is in you and mee to accomplish their requestes. And thus beinge bold to trooble you, I commytt you to God, wisshinge to you longe life with helth. Boughton, this xiijth of Februarie, 1588.

Your asswerid frend,

E. MOUNTAGU

[fo. 142b] [Also in Montagu's hand:] To the Righte Worshipfull and his verye good frend, Sir Richard Knightly, knighte, these.

[Traces of seal]

81. [fo. 165a] [PRIVY SEALS: DEFECTS AND ABATEMENTS. 1588/9.][3]

[Enclosed with No. 80]

Northampton shire. A declaration of the Privie Seales within the said Cownty, with the defectes and abatements as folowethe:-

Sir Thomas Tresham, 1li.; Thomas Bawer, xxvli.; Edmund Foster, xxvli.; Thomas Harby, 1li.; Richard Chitwood, 1li., [be[i]] charged [and paid[i]] in other Counties, which are requiereth to be dischargd of without supply [out, not dwelling in the County[d]].

Anthony Stratford, xxvli.; John Pee, xxvli.; Richard Smith, 1li. These dwelling in other Counties.

Thomas Humfry, xxvli.; Thomas Freear, xxvli.; William Paynter, xxvli.;

---

[1] See **81**.
[2] This "kalender" is not extant.
[3] All the names in this document are in column.

Roberte Andro [gen.*i*], xxv*li*.; Larance Eton, l*li*.; Henry Marson, xxv*li*.;
Hugh Yeomans, xxv*li*.; William Wickins, xxv*li*.; Symon Brookes, xxv*li*.;
William Howse, xxv*li*.; Edward Love, xxv*li*.; Michaell Chambers, xxv*li*.;
Mathew Glover, xxv*li*.; Thomas Onely [gen*i*] xxv*li*.; Richard Gray [gen'*i*]
xxv*li*.; John Towers, xxv*li*.; Roger Hasken, xxv*li*.; John Manning, xxv*li*.;
Morrice Myles, l*li*.; [Edward Bacon gen'*d*] xxv*li*.

> [*The names in the above paragraph are bracketed, and against
> the bracket is written in the margin:*]

These [we thincke*d*] [we thincke of our discrecions*i*] [to*d*] be insufficient
as are well knowne to the wholl Country.

> [*In the left-hand margin opposite the above column of names is
> the following list in a different (unclerkly) hand:*]

Sir Robert Lane, knight, l*li*.; John Lenton [esqr.*i*] l*li*.; John Humfry
[gen*i*], xxv*li*.; John Wstis[?], xxv*li*.; John Clementes, xxv*li*.; Thomas Clark,
gen', xxv*li*.; William Eston, xxv*li*.; Georg Walker, l*li*.; Morice Palmer [gen*i*],
xxv*li*.; Tho. Palmer [gen*i*], xxv*li*.; Tho. Tawyte [gen*i*] xxv*li*.; Edmund
Aprice, xxv*li*.; Richard Curtis, xxv*li*.; Edward Bacon [*blank*].

> [*The main list continues:*]

Thomas Croswell, l*li*.; John Hensman, l*li*.; John Brian, l*li*.; [*in the
margin:*] these [iij discharged*d*] [be abated*i*] by your honours letters.

> [*In the left hand margin opposite the above three names:*]

Larenc Baly, xxv*li*.; Tho: Stiles, xxv*li*.; John Wildbore, xxv*li*.; Wm
Kirkham [xxv*li.d*] [l*li.i*].

> [*The main list continues:*]

Robert Hurste, l*li*.; . xxv*li*.; Willm Baldwin, l*li*.; . xxv*li*.; Georg Sherley,
C*li*.; . l*li*.; . xxv*li*.; John Isham, esq., l*li*.; xxv*li*.; Edward Haslerigg, l*li*.; . xxv*li*.

> [*Against the above 5 names, which are bracketed, is written:*]
> These be overcharged and abated by our discrecions. [*Note that
> the lower sums against each name, and also Sherley's, Isham's
> and Haslerigg's names are in the same hand as the marginal note
> above, as also is the following note in the left hand margin
> here:*] These be discharged by your Honores comaund.

[*The main list continues:*] Henry Tailor alias Paris, xxv*li*., dead;
Richard Knighte, xxv*li*. dead.

Sir Richard Knightley and his son requir that favour which other
Deputy Leaftenantes haue in other Counties, his charge and expenses
considered. Sir Edward Mountagu. [*The sum opposite his name has been
torn or rubbed off, as also have one or two words below Montagu's name*]
[Total] ij*Cli*.

[Summa : ix*C*iij*xx*xv*li.d*]

[*fo*. 165b] Summa totalis of the Privie Seales that her Majestie
requirethe in the said Countye comethe to V M *li*.
Sum of the reprises, deductions, abatementes and paimentes is
j*M*viij*C*l *li*.

So remaineth to the Queenes Majestie to be paid out of our Country,
iij M *li*., if it please your Lordshippe to grante the abatement accordinge

to this particuler, and j^cl *li.* to be abated on suche as your Lordshippe shall thinck moste meet.

82. [*fo.* 138a] [LETTER. MONTAGU TO KNIGHTLEY. 15 February, 1588/9.]

[*Holograph*]

After my verie hartye commendacions. I perceive by your letters that you haue beene with my Lorde Chauncellor and my Lorde Treasorer aboute the Privie Seales, bicause theire is many of them directed to some verie poore men and others of meane hability, wherewith they find them selues muche greeved bicause theire betters are not charged therewith, and do thincke that it is doone by your certifycatt and myne, soe as they dailie repaire to mee to bee eased thereof; which, as you knowe, I can noe way pleasure more then to certefy his Lordship, as of late by letters vnto his Lordship and your selfe will appeare.

The somme that theire Lordships will haue certen out of this County is iiij^M *li.* The odd five hundred you say they are contented to abbate of such as you and I shall thincke moste fytt, and that wee should name them vnder our handes. If you will haue this poore man Mannyng to be one, then the seven in your postscript must haue one abated for your diuision.

Theire hath beene with mee to be discharged and releeved since I wrote vnto you such as shalbee named herevnder wrytten, and the some of five hundred poundes will pleasure very fewe consideringe the number that is greeved, excepte it shall please theire good Lordes to charge men of greater possessions and welth as bee not towched, where for your better memory I sente you the names of xl^{tie}, and you may add to those William Scarre of Stamford Barron and Bryan Penney of Peterborow, so as out of the number of xl^{tc}ij, the beste of them may supplie and ease theire neighbors if soe it may stand with theire Lordshippes good pleasures.

If you and I with the Justices had made certificatt as they did in other Counties, halfe this trubble would haue beene saved, bycause if theire bee a supplie they muste haue Privie Seales, and those that have receued the others that [shallⁱ] bee discharged muste bee returned. Thus wisshing to you longe life with helth, I leaue you to God. Boughton, this xvth of Februarie, 1588.

Your asswerid frend,

E. MOUNTAGU

[*Continued in Montagu's hand:*] Roberte Wingfeild, esquier, l *li.*; George Lynne, esquier, l *li.*; Frances Ashbie, esquier, l *li.*; Edward Haslerigg, being of small frehold and a great charge of children, l*li.*; John Wildbore, xxv *li.*; John Clementes of Oundell, xxv*li.*; Edward Knight of Piddington, xxv *li.*

[*Postscript:*]
I do not set downe any kalendar according to your request for the abating of the v^C *li* vntill I here from you of theire Lordshippes further pleasures. Theire muste bee a supply had or ells theire wilbe contynnuall crying out, and so you may signify to theire Lordships.

[*fo.* 141b] [*In Montagu's hand:*] To the Righte Wurshipfull my verie good frend, Sir Richard Knightley, knight, at his lodginge in the Woolstable neere Westminster, these.

[*Traces of seal*]

83. [*fo.* 139a]   [LETTER.   MONTAGU   TO   KNIGHTLEY. 17 February, 1588/9.]

[*Holograph*]

Sir, I haue wrytten vnto my very good Lord, the Lord Chauncellor, and haue sente you the same hereinclosed which, after you haue redd and thincke good to deliuer it, then I praye you seale it, for that you and I can make noe perfect callender excepte wee may haue a true note of the somes wherewith euery man is charged that hath had Privie Seales deliuered vnto them, which hadd, wee mighte easily releaue somme of our neighbors if [the^i] his Lordship shall like thereof, as by [his^d] [my^i] letters doth appeare. [If certificatt^d]
Thus [wissh^d] with my hartie commendacions I leaue you to God. Boughton, the xvijth of Februarie, 1588.
                    Your asswrid frend,

E. MOUNTAGU

Theire is a scedule also in my Lordes letter of such as would bee discharged and eased.

[*Postscript:*]
I am credibly enformed that Lyncolne shire is rated but [at^i] iij^M v^C *li.*, which is thrise so bigg as Northampton shire, and a number of gentlemen of greate worship and welth, and to haue this Shire charged with iiij^M *li.* wee haue iuste cause to bee greeved thereat. Therefore it were not a misse for you to emparte the same to theire good Lordshippes, for if they hold that mynd, theire hand is very heauy vppon vs. The generall losse that hath beene this yere in our cuntry both by hay and cattell, besides the charges of the seruice considered, hath impouerished the cuntry, and the complaint is not without greate cause.

[*fo.* 140b] To the Righte Worshipfull Sir Richard Knightlie, knighte, geue these, at his lodginge in the Rounde Woolstaple, neere Westminster.

[*Traces of seal*]

84. [*fo.* 132a] [LETTER. HATTON TO KNIGHTLEY AND MONTAGU. 16 March, 1588/9.]

After my very hartie commendacions. Whereas the Countie of Northampton hathe lately ben charged by Privie Seale with the loane of five thowsande poundes [to be made¹] vnto her Majestie towardes a supplie of charge for the necessarie defence of the Realme, and that by informacion receaved from you I am made to vnderstande that the same rate imposed vppon the Shiere is founde to be greater then it maye conveniently beare, especially the rate considered, which is required of others [*sic*] Shieres of the Realme, being of farre greater habilitie then owres, I haue herevppon had conference with my Lordes of the Councell, as being desierous to helpe to ease our countrie by all convenient meanes, so farforthe as maye stande with our diuties in shewing our readines to yelde her Highnes all the ayde we can vp[on eve]rie¹ occasion; and in thende it hathe ben [. . . . . .] Lordshippes, that an abatement and deduccion sh[. . .] one thowsande fyve hundred poundes owte of the whole s[. . .] tnowsande poundes before demaunded, so [. . .]be rendred into her Majesties cofers the intiere sum [. . .] thowsande fyve hundred poundes, according to which summe you are to [. . . .] your leavies in your severall divisions, and no farther, notwithstanding anie other order given vnto you heretofore.

And the deduccion so to be made is referred to your good discrecions, to defalke the same where moste neede shall be, that suche chiefly maye be eased therby as ar leaste hable to yelde anie such contribucion of loane within either of your said divisions.

Whereof not dowbting but you will haue an especiall regarde, and take order withall for the leavieng of this summe required with all the speede you can, I bidde you bothe very hartiely fare well. From the Courte at Whytehall, the xvjth of Marche, 1588.

Your very loving assured frende,

" CHR : HATTON, Canc. "

[*Postscript:*]
Where you shall see that summe ar to be esaed, but maye beare sume parte of the loane, according [to?] the rates of 100, 50 and 25 *li.* sett [doune¹] vppon aduertisement thereof from you, newe Priuie Seale shalbe directed vnto them accordingly.

Sir Richard Knightley
Sir Edward Mountague

[*fo.* 135b] To the Right Worshipfull my very good frendes, Sir Richarde Knightley and Sir Edwarde Mountague, knightes, her Majesties Deputie Lieutenauntes of the Countie of Northampton, and to either of them, give theise.

¹ Roughly a semicircular piece has been torn off the edge of the folio where the seal was applied, leaving two or three words missing at the end of this and the following six lines of the MS.

85. [*fo.* 163a] The Defectes [and Abatements*i*] in the West Diuision. [1588/9?]

NORTHAMPTON TOWNE
  Thomas Creswell, l*li.*
  John Hensman, l*li.*
  John Brian, l*li.*
  Abated to xxv*li.* a peece.
  Thomas Humfry, xxv *li.*, not hable.
  Thomas Freear, xxv*li.*, not hable.
  William Painter, xxv*li.*, not hable.
NEWBOTTLE HUNDRED
  Roberte Androe, xxv*li.*, not hable.
  Larance Eton, [xx*d*] l*li.*, not hable.
  Henry Marson, xxv*li.*, not hable.
  Hugh Yeomans, xxv*li.*, not hable.
  Richard Knighte, xxv*li.*, is dead.
CLEYLEY HUNDRED
  William Wickins, xxv*li.*, not hable.
NORTON HUNDRED
  Thomas Harby, l*li.*, paid in Midlesex.
  Anthonie Stratford, xxv*li.*, [charged*d*] [gon*i*] into Glocester shire to dwell.
  [Greg' Sherley*d*]
TOCESTER HUNDRED
  Simon Brookes, xxv*li.*, not hable.
  William Howse, xxv*li.*, not hable.
SUTTON HUNDRED
  Richard Chitwood, l*li.*, charged in Buck shire.
  Edward Loue, xxv*li.*, not hable.
  Michaell Chambers, xxv*li.*, not hable.
  Henrie Tailor alias Paris, xxv*li.*, is dead.
  Georg' Sherly, esq., c*li.*, abated to l*li.*
SPELLO HUNDRED
  Robert Hurse, charged at l*li.*, abated to xxv*li.*
  Mathew Glover, xxv*li.*, not hable.
WARDON HUNDRED
  William Baldwin, l*li.*, abated to xxv*li.*
FAWSLEY HUNDRED
  Thomas Onely, xxv*li.*, not hable.
  Richard Gray, xxv*li.*, not hable.
  John Towers, xxv*li.*, not hable.
WINBERSLEY HUNDRED
  Roger Hasken, xxv*li.*, not hable.
  John Manninge, xxv*li.*, not hable.
GILSBOROW HUNDRED
  Morice Miles, l*li.*, not hable.

  Summa: abatements or defectes, ix[c]l *li.*

86. [*fo.* 164a]   THE SUPPLIES IN THE WEST DIUISION. [1588/9?][1]

NORTHAMPTON TOWNE
   [*blank*]
CLEYLEY HUNDRED
   John Mariot of Ashton, gen'
NEWBOTTLE HUNDRED
   Valentyne Gregorie of Harlston, gen'
   Roberte Britten of Teeton, gen'
NORTON HUNDRED
   John Androes of Whitleberey
WARDON HUNDRED
   Roberte Wasshington of Sulgraue
   William Howell of Sulgraue
   Anthonie Humfry of Sulgraue
SUTTON HUNDRED
   Foolke Odill of [Che Chacombe*d*] Thenford.
   Richard Foxe of Chacombe
   Thomas Emeley of Helmeden
   Edward Thorne alias Dorne of Siersham
SPELLO HUNDRED
   Larance Manley of Spratton
FAWSLEY HUNDRED
   [Roberte Harison*d*]
   William Glouer of Heleden
   Thomas Ere of Farthingston
WIMBERSLEY HUNDRED
   Thomas Lolam of Houghton
GILSBOROW HUNDRED
   Mr. Cave of Stanford [*altered from* Stamford], esquier

87. [*fo.* 143a]   [LIST OF PRIVY SEALS FOR THE WEST DIVISION,
4 April, 1589.]

The West Division of the County of Northampton.

Quarto Aprilis, 1589.
Receaued of Rowland White, the daie and yeare aboue written, these
Privy Seales following, being discharged by the Lorde Lieutenant of the
said County, viz: -[2]

. Thomas Onely, gent.	.	.	.	.	.	xxv *li.*
. Hugh Chamberlaine	.	.	.	.	.	xxv *li.*
. Robert Andrewe	.	.	.	.	.	xxv *li.*

[1] This list seems to be complementary to the preceding document, giving here the names of those expected to pay up.
[2] Each name in this list is ticked, the first 22 with a dot, and the last 7 with a stroke of the pen. Thomas Onely to Thomas Humfrye are bracketed. Sir R. Knightley and Valentine Knightley are bracketed. The dots against these last two names are vague and indeterminate.

	. John Mannyng	xxv *li.*
	. Michaell Chambers	xxv *li.*
	. Morrice Myles	1 *li.*
	. John Towers	xxv *li.*
	. Hugh Yeomans	xxv *li.*
vnhable	. Henry Marson	xxv *li.*
	. Symon Brookes	xxv *li.*
	. Lawrence Eaton	1 *li.*
	. Edward Love	xxv *li.*
	. Richard Grey, gent.	xxv *li.*
	. Roger Haskyn [*altered from* Haskell] .	xxv *li.*
	. William Wyckens	xxv *li.*
	. Matthew Glover	xxv *li.*
	. William Howse	xxv *li.*
	. William Paynter	xxv *li.*
	. Thomas Humfrye	xxv *li.*

Deputy Lieutenant { . Sir Richard Knightley, knight . . . 1 *li.*
and his sonne   { . Valentyne Knightley, esq. . . . . 1 *li.*

/ George Sherley, esquior .	. c *li.* abated to 1 *li.*
/ John Bryan	1 *li.* abated to
/ Thomas Creswell . .	1 *li.* xxv *li*
/ John Hensman . . .	1 *li.* a peece.
/ Richard Chittwood, esq.	1 *li.* payd elswhere
/ Anthony Stratford	xxv *li.*

gon out of the County

/ Henry Tayler alias Parrys . xxv *li.* mort[uus]

[Total] 28

"THO: KERY"

88. [*fo.* 133a] [LETTER. HATTON TO KNIGHTLEY AND MONTAGU. 16 May, 1589.]

After my very hartie commendacions. Whereas summe fewe weekes past I receaved a certificate from you of suche gentlemen and other of our Countie as wer to be charged with loanes of money vnto her Majestie by Privie Seale, by which certificate it appeerethe that the intier summe of three thousande poundes sholde be aunswered vnto her Majestie owte of the whole Countie, wherein I cowlde not before signifie vnto you what wolde be determined towching the allowaunce or acceptacion of that summe; theise shall be to lett you vnderstande that it is nowe resolved by my Lordes that the said summe of three thowsande poundes (the [smallenes*d*] [povertie*i*] of our Shiere considered) shall suffize and be accepted, for the full loane of money that our said Shiere is to be charged with, vppon the [late*i*] Privie Seales which wer directed into the same.

It is therefore required of you that with all convenient speede you cawse the said summe of iij^Mli. to be aunswered into her Majesties Exchequer. And incase in the leavieng thereof, you shall fynde anie (which ar particularly charged with anie parte of the said loane) vnhable to performe the same, that then according to your discrecions you name vnto vs summe others in their places fitt to supplie those loanes to thende newe Privie Seales may be directed vnto them, as shall appertaine.

Moreover if you shall fynde anie of those that you iudge sufficient to aunswer anie of those loanes, slacke and remisse in the payment of the same, you ar also with lyke speede to certifie vnto vs their names, that such further order may be taken with them as to their Lordshippes shall be thowghte conveniente.

And herein prayeng you very earnestly there may be no defaulte, I bidde you bothe very hartiely fare well. From London, the xvjth of Maye, 1589.

Your very loving assured frende,

" CHR : HATTON, Canc. "

Sir Richard Knightley
Sir Edward Mountague

[*fo.* 134b] To my very loving good frendes, Sir Richarde Knightley and Sir Edwarde Mountague, knightes, Deputie Lieutenantes of the Countie of Northampton, and to either of them, give theise.

[*Traces of seal*]

89. [*fo.* 149a] [LETTER. HATTON TO KNIGHTLEY AND MONTAGU. 19 May, 1589.][1]

After my very hartie commendacions. I sende you here enclosed a letter[2] receaved from my Lordes for the newe trayning and putting in readines the forces of our Shiere according to former direccions. My desier is that with all carefull regarde you see the same in everie respecte duely performed, my selfe being earnestly required and willed thereunto, as by the contentes of their Lordshippes said letter shall appeere vnto you.

The thinges you are chiefly to looke vnto ar theise: that your bandes maye consiste of good and hable men for service, either by former experience or for their aptnes to be browghte thereunto by exercise of trayning; as also that their leaders, lieutenantes and other officers maye be knowen vnto you to be men fitt to take those charges vppon them. I referre all to your good discrecions, hoping the same shall be so done as bothe her Majestie and my L[ordes] maye perceave our dutifull c[are] and regarde in the accomplishement of theise their d[ireccio]ns, and of anie thing required besydes, according to the[ir fo]rmer instruccions.

You ar lykewyse to certifie the state of the forces of the Shiere as vppon the reviewe they shall be founde nowe to be according to the postscripte of their Lordshippes letter.

And evenso reposing my selfe vppon yo[ur] frendlie good endevoures

---

[1] A piece has been torn off the edge of this letter.
[2] The letter is not in this collection.

herein, I bidde you bothe very hartiely fare well. From the Cowrte att Whytehall, the xixth of Maye, 1589.

Your very assured loving frende,
" CHR : HATTON, Canc. "

Sir Richard Knightley
Sir Edward Mountague

[fo. 156b] To my very loving good frendes, Sir Richarde Knightley and Sir Edwarde Mountague, knightes, Deputie Lieutenauntes of the Countie of Northampton, and to either of them.

[*Further endorsement in another hand:*] Bee it knowne vnto all men by these presentes.[1]
[*Traces of seal*]

90. [fo. 144a]   [LETTER. MONTAGU TO KNIGHTLEY, 16 June, 1589.]

[*Holograph*]

Sir,

Whereas by letters from my Lord Chauncellor dated the xvjth [day] of May, this County is charged with the som of three thowsand pound, and yt is requyred of you and mee that wyth all convenient speede wee cause the said som to bee aunswered into her Majesties Exchequer, wherevppon I directed out bills the xxjth of May vnto all such as were charged by Pryuy Seale to make speedy paymente thereof beeffore the firste of June; notwithstandinge, theyre slacknes is such as I thought good to aduertyse you bicause the greatest defalt resteth in your diuision, as shall appeare vnto you by their names in a scedule hereinclosed, desyring you to take such order that the partyes may make speedy payment to my handes, for otherwise both you and I shalbee compelled to aduertise his good Lordship of theire slacknes. For if wee shallbee enforced to certefye a new supply for the aunswering of the said somme which muste bee paide by this County, it wilbee nothing pleasing to our cuntreymen, and especially to your diuision, for theire is not aboue vj or vij at the moste but haue made payment to my handes within this diuisyon.

I haue taken vew of the bandes that serued the laste yere and haue had the captaynes with mee, who, as I perceyue, are willinge to contynue theire chardge. Som defaultes theire bee, but of noe great waighte, as losse of cotes and some armor and shott, for which I haue charged the partyes to bee refurnished againe. And as for want of men in theire seuerall bandes, I haue made a new supply acordingly. Thereffore what certyficatt you will make towchinge this seruice, I pray you drawe yt downe and I will ioyne with you in certefyinge thereof, or whether you thinck yt better to stay the certyfying vntill the horsmen haue beene vewed, and then to certefy the state of the wholl force of the County. I desyre to know who shall haue the leading of them, bicause I thinck Mr. Lane will not take that chardge vppon him, consydering his place.

And thus with my verye hartye commendacions to you and your

---

[1] An attempt has been made to erase the last four words.

honorable Ladie, I wishe to you and yours longe lyffe with healthe. Barnewell, this xvjth of June, 1589.

Your asswerid frend,

E. MOUNTAGU

[fo. 147b] [In Montagu's hand:] To the Right Wurshipfull and his very good frend, Sir Rychard Knightlye, knight, theise.

91. [fo. 145a] [THE SCHEDULE OF THE DEFAULTERS IN THE MATTER OF THE LOAN. June, 1589.][1]

[Enclosed with No. 90]

Samuell Davers	xxv *li.*
William Dormar	1 *li.*
James Kendricke	xxv *li.*
Anthonie Morgan	xxv *li.*
John Blinco	xxv *li.*
Roberte Creswell	xxv *li.*
John Browne	xxv *li.*
Patricke Lyle	xxv *li.*
Edward Cope	1 *li.*
Fraunces Foxely	1 *li.*
Anthonie Stratford	xxv *li.* out of the country
Fyrmyn Russell	xxv *li.*
Thomas Leeson	xxv *li.*
Roberte Harloe	xxv *li.*
Edward Knighte	xxv *li.*
Stephen Harvey	xxv *li.*
Hugh Chamberlen	xxv *li.* discharged
John Neale	1 *li.*
Thomas Croswell	xxv *li.*
John Hensman	xxv *li.*
John Bryan	xxv *li.*
John Kirkland	xxv *li.*
William Rainsford	xxv *li.*
John Mercer	xxv *li.*
Sir George Farmor, knight . . . [xxv *li.*^a] 1 *li.*
Eusabie Isham	1 *li.*
John Billing	xxv *li.*
Richard Smith	1 *li.*
Frances Worley	xxv *li.*
William Watkin	xxv *li.*
Thomas Robins	xxv *li.*

Summa ix^Clxxv *li.* [*sic*]

[1] With the exception of the marginal notes, this document is in Montagu's hand.

92. [*fo*. 157a] [LETTER. HATTON TO CECIL, KNIGHTLEY, MONTAGU AND SIR GEORGE FERMOR. 5 September, 1590.]

After my very hartie commendacions. Her Majestie, fynding it very necessarie that a generall reviewe sholde be hadde of her forces within the Realme, hathe willed that present direccion be given therein to her Lieutenauntes Generall of everie Shiere and that speciall care be taken in the due execucion thereof, as shall appeere vnto you by the letter here enclosed[1] directed vnto me from my Lordes in that behalfe. The charge and commaundement which I receave herein (as you see) is very straighte. I doe therefore earnestly requier you presently vppon the receipte hereof to enter into this busines, and that pervsing particularly sundr[y] your former instruccions, you see everie thing performed in the best manner according to their Lordshippes presente direccion, consisting principally in this: that perfecte musters be made of all the forces of the Shiere within the tyme prescribed; as also that all defectes whatsoever, of captaines, officers, soldiours, horse, armour, weapon and what ever ells, you may be carefully provided for and supplied in tyme; as lykewyse that you sende perfecte bookes thereof as particularly as shall be meete, according to the forme heretofore prescribed vnto you.

And herein earnestly prayeng you there maye be no defaulte for suche speciall respectes of diutie and otherwyse as by former letters I haue towched vnto you, I bidde you very hartiely fare well. From Drayton, the vth of September, 1950.

Your very loving assured frende,

"CHR: HATTON, Canc."

Sir Thomas Cecill
Sir Richard Knightley
Sir Edwarde Mountague
Sir George Farmer

[*fo*. 162b] To the Right Worshipfull my very good frendes, Sir Thomas Cecill, Sir Richarde Knightley, Sir Edwarde Montague and Sir George Farmer, knightes, and to everie of them, give theise.

[*Traces of seal*]

93. [*fo*. 12a] [LETTER. LORD BURGHLEY TO KNIGHTLEY. 5 February, 1590/1.]

After my verie hartie commendacions. This bearer, Thomas Brickett, hath informed me that he hath lately purchased of hir Majestie 2 tenementes lying within Morton Pinckney, and that you haue certein evidence concerning the said tenementes in your custodie. Wherefore, vppon his request made vnto me, I have thought good to require you

---

[1] The letter is not in this collection.

that you will deliuer the said evidence vnto him, so that they concerne nothing els but the said 2 tenementes so purchased of hir Majestie, for that therebye hir Majestie can receyve no preiudice and that of right they are to go with the lande. Otherwise, if they concerne any other lande of hir Majesties, or that you have any reasonable cause to retayne them, my meaning is not to move you therein, for that, if they appertyne in any sort to hir Majestie, they are not to be deliuered without order of the Courte.

So fare you hartely well. From Westminster, this vth of Februarie, 1590.

Your verie lovinge frend,

" W. BURGHLEY "

Sir Richard Knightley

[*fo.* 153b] To my verie lovinge frend, Sir Richard Knightley, knighte.

[*Traces of seal*]

94. [*fo.* 151a] [LETTER. HATTON TO KNIGHTLEY, MONTAGU AND SIR GEORGE FERMOR. 9 February, 1590/1.]

After my very hartie commendacions. Fynding, by letters lately directed vnto me from my Lordes of the Counsell, her Majesties especiall care that the former orders restrayning the common and disordered killing and eating of fleshe in the tyme of Lent sholde in everie parte of the Realme be putt in due execucion and observed this yeare with more care and diligence then hathe ben vsed heretofore, as noting therein summe former remisnes and negligence in those who had that charge committed vnto them, I haue therefore thowghte good hereby very earnestly to praye and requier you to see the said orders in everie respecte duely and strictly executed, agreable to her Majesties expectacion and the speciall charge we receave therein from their Lordshippes for the avoyding of the lyke blame and imputacion hereafter. And to thende you maye the better vnderstande their Lordshippes direccion therein, I haue herewith sent vnto you the copie of their letter[1] nowe last written vnto me in that behalfe, as also certaine copies of the said orders imprinted, which you ar to bestowe and publishe in suche sorte, as for the better observacion of the same generally you shall thincke to be moste convenient.

Wherein I dowbte not but you will vse the greater care and regarde, in that you shall perceave howe earnestly it is required at my handes that I sholde take order therein accordingly. In which, as I repose my selfe chiefly vppon your good endevoures, so shall I haue cawse greatly to thancke you for the same. And evenso I bidde you very hartiely fare well. From London, the ixth of Februarie, 1590.

Your very loving assured frende,

" CHR: HATTON, Canc. "

[1] For the copy of the privy council's letter, see **95**. There is no copy of the printed orders in this collection.

Sir Richard Knightley
Sir Edward Mountague
Sir George Farmer

[*fo.* 154b] To the Right Worshipfull my very loving frendes, Sir Richarde Knightley, Sir Edwarde Mountague and Sir George Farmer, knightes, her Majesties Deputie Lieutenauntes of the Countie of Northampton, give theise.

[*Part of Hatton's armorial seal*]

95. [*fo.* 150a] [LETTER. THE COUNCIL TO HATTON. 7 February, 1590/1.][1]

[*Copy. Enclosed with No. 94*]

After our right harty commendacions to your good Lordshippe. Her [Majestie, for] the care she hath yerely had to restrayne the common and disordered killing and eating of fleshe in the tyme of Lent, aswell within the Cittie of London as in other partes of the Realme, hath ben pleased that the former orders sholde be renued and newly increased and putt in execucion this yere for the lyke restrainte,[2] the rather in respecte of the deathe [and] losse of sheepe [and] other cattell happened by reason of the great vnreasonable drowthe of the laste [somer[d]] spring and summer. B[y] whose speciall direccion we haue sent herewith to your Lordshippe certaine [co]pies of the said orders imprinted, which her Majestie would haue to be published, putt in execucion and obserued in all the chiefe townes [and] places of the Countie vnder your Lordshippes Lieuetenauncie in all respectes as in the said orders is expressed.

To which ende your Lordshippe shall do well to giue order to your Deputies, and to all the Justices of Peace and to the officers of all corporate townes or exempte places, that they see the said orders or so muche of them duely and diligently kepte and obserued as may well in your discreations be putt in execucion within theire seuerall iurisdiccions.

And bycause there may be manie sicke and weake persons within the same that cannott withowte daunger feede on fishe, you may, in the Shiere townes and suche other corporate and markett townes as you or your Deputies and the Justices ioyntly shall thincke meete, cawse summe one [but]cher to be permitted to kill and sell fleshe to such only as s[hall] haue lycense to eate the same, and to none others, observing a[ll] condicions by bondes, as in the orders are mencioned.

The principa[ll] and needfull pointes thereof wee praye you to see or cawse to be obserued with more care and diligence then heretofore hath ben in the lyke, whereby the preiudice and hurte growing to the Realme by the common and disordered killing and eating of fleshe in the tymes

---

[1] The edge of the MS. has been rubbed off in places, and words or parts thereof have been conjecturally supplied.

[2] For the orders sent out in February 1590, see H.M.C., *Montagu of Beaulieu*, p. 22.

prohibited, to the contempte of the lawes and of her Majesties aucthoritye, m[ay] be avoyded.

Whereunto her Majestie expectethe that summe extraordyn[arie] regarde be had att this tyme, aswell by your Lordshippe as by the Justices [of] Peace and officers within theire seuerall rules, as they will aunsw[ere] the truste reposed in them, and to eschewe the daunger of her Ma[jesties] indignacion.

And so nott doubting butt your Lordshippes example in observing [the] same in your owne familye, and in shewing a care to haue the said orders well and duely executed, will be a good occasion vnto the rest, to haue the[m] the better to perfourme as muche as to their duetye appertaynethe, wee bydd you right hartely farewell. From the Cowrte att Richmond, the vijth of Februarie, 1590.

Your Lordshippes verie loving frendes,

JO: CANT.   CHR: HATTON, Canc.   W. BURLEIGHE   C. HOWARDE
HOUNSDON   COBHAM   T. BUCKHURSTE   T. HENEAGE

[fo. 155b] To our very good Lorde, the Lord Chaunccllor of Englande, her Majesties Lieutenaunte of the Countie of Northampton.

96. [fo. 167b] [LETTER. SIR EUSEBY ANDREW TO SIR WILLIAM TATE. 8 December, 1614.]

Worthy Cozen,

It is our Lord Lieuetennantes[1] pleasure to haue as large a certificate as hath bin heretofore deliuered vnto him, the which he did longe since expecte, being to aquaint the Lordes withall proceedings on Sabathday last. I haue sent yow herewith a coppy of that certificate which was sent him the last yeare, and alsoe a foule drafte of that which I conceaue wee are nowe to send him, not as yet in any sorte perfected.[2] My desire is that yow woold be pleased to write your opinion what is (as yow thincke) moste fitte to be done in it.

The Lordes alsoe (as farre as I can learne) doe expecte a [certif^d] particuler certificate of the severall summs that any man of any fashion doth giue, not concludinge them vpp in one lumpe with the toune where in they liue, but seuerally by themselues. Wherfore I hould it not amisse if wee coold agree of a meetinge (togither with the collectour) to frame a certificate, and not leaue it to be done by the collectour alone, whoe will not incurre the least displeasure in this buisines, as he did tell me, meeting him at Sir Arthures[3] when I came from London. The sooner we dispatche the better it wilbe, for it is daily expected and allmost all Countries haue sent vp somewhat that doe intende to giue any thinge at all.

Thus with my best service to my Lady, and loue to your selfe,

I reste, your assured freind and louinge cozen,

"EUSEBIE ANDREUE"

[1] Thomas Cecil, Earl of Exeter.
[2] For the certificate, see **97**; the "foule drafte" is presumably **98**.
[3] Sir Arthur Throckmorton, who served with Tate as a deputy lieutenant for Northants.

Norton, the 8th of December, 1614.

[*fo.* 166a] To his assured freind and louinge Cozen, Sir William Tate, knight, at Delapre, these bee d[elivere]d.

97. [*fo.* 166b] [CERTIFICATE OF ARMOUR AND WEAPONS IN THE WEST DIVISION. 1613.][1]

[Enclosed with No. 96]

Hundreds	Townes	Cor[slettes]	Musk[ettes]	Cal[ivers]
FAULESLY	Euerdons	1	0	1
	Ashby Legers	1	0	1
	Killesby	1	1	2
1	Welton	2	1	1
	Stowes	1	0	1
1	Branson	2	0	0
	Weedon Beck	1	1	1
	Lichburrow	1	0	1
	Preston Capes	1	0	1
	Farthingston [Charwelton[d]]	1	0	0
	Charweton [*sic*]	0	0	1
	Badby	1	0	1
	Newnham	1	0	0
	Barby cum Only	1	0	2
	Hellidon cum Catesby	1	0	1
	Dodford	1	0	0
1	Stauerton	2	0	0
	Norton	0	1	0
1	Daventrye	3	1	4
		22	5	18

[Hundreds]	[Townes]	[Corslettes]	[Muskettes]	[Calivers]
GUILESBUR	Weshaddon	1[2]	1	0[3]
	Creatons	1	0	1
	Cottesbroke	1	0	0[4]
	Wynwick	1	0	0
	Welford	1[5]	1	1
1+	Bugby longa	2	1	2
1+	Gulesbur:	2	0[6]	2[7]
	Crick	1	1	2
	Cley Coaton	1	0	1
1	Lilborne	2	0	0

[1] Cf. the lists of men, armour and weapons in *M.B.S.*, pp. 129-66.
[2] Altered from " 2 "   [4] Altered from " 1 "   [6] Altered from " 2 "
[3] Altered from " 1 "   [5] Altered from " 2 "   [7] Altered from " 3 "

[Hundreds]	[Townes]	[Corslettes]	[Muskettes]	[Calivers]
	Navesby	1	0	1
[1^d]	Yeluertoft	2	0	0
	Thornby	1	1[1]	0
	Ashby Leger [sic, for Cold Ashby]	1	0	1
	Stanford	1	0	1[2]
	Watford	1	0	2
		20	5[3]	14[4]

[Hundreds]	[Townes]	[Corslettes]	[Muskettes]	[Calivers]
WARDEN	Chip[ping] Warden	1	0	1
	Edgcot	1	0	0
	Woodford cum [membris]	1	0	1
	Eydon	1	1	1
	Ashton le Walls	1	0	1
1	Boddingtons	2	0	1
	Gritworth	1	0	0
	Bifeild	1	0	1
	Sulgrave	0	2[5]	0
		9	3[6]	6

[Hundreds]	[Townes]	[Corslettes]	[Muskettes]	[Calivers]
NEWBOTLE	East Hadon	1	0	2
	Harleston	1	1	1
1	Bringtons	2	0	2
	Ravensthorpe and Tekon	2	0	0
	Kislingbury	1	0	2[7]
	Duston and St. Ja[meses] End	1	0	2
	Vpton	0	1	0
	Bramptons	2	0	1
	Brochole	0	0	1
	Flower	1	1	0
1	Bugbrok	2	0	1
	Heifordes	1	0	1
	Harpole	1	0	1
	Whilton	1	0	0
	Dallington	1	0	1
		17	4	15[8]

[1] Altered from " 0 "
[2] Altered from " 2 "
[3] Altered from " 7 "
[4] Altered from " 18 "
[5] Altered from " 3 "
[6] Altered from " 4 "
[7] Altered from " 3 "
[8] Altered from " 16 "

[Hundreds]	[Townes]	[Corslettes]	[Muskettes]	[Calivers]
SPELHO 1	Kingesthorp	2	0	1
	Billing Magna	1	0	1
	Billing Parva	1	0	0
	Ouerston	1	1	0
1	Moulton	2	0	2
	Buckon [for Boughton]	1	0	0
	Spratton	1	1	1[1]
	Weston Favell	1	1	0
	Pisford	1	1[2]	1
	Abbington	1	0	1
		12	4	7[3]

[Hundreds]	[Townes]	[Corslettes]	[Muskettes]	[Calivers]
WIMERSLEY	Milton	1	0	1
	Blisworth	1	0	1
	Courtenhall	1	0	0+1
	Wooton	1	0	1
	Quinton	1	0	0
	Houghton Magna	1	0	1
	Houghton Parva	1	0	1+1
	Rothersthorp	1	0	1
	Collingtre	1	0	0
	Brafield	1	1	0+1
	Cogenho	1	0	0
	Whiston	1	0	0
	Castle Ashby	0	0	2
	Yardly cum Denton	1	1	0
	Grindon	1	0	0
	Piddington & Haccleton	1	0	1
	Horton	0	1	0
	Hardingstone cum Cotton	2	0	1
		17	3	10[4]

[Hundreds]	[Townes]	[Corslettes]	[Muskettes]	[Calivers]
NORTON	Bradden	1	0	1
	Weston and Weedon	1	0	1
	Slapton	0	1	0
	Maidford cum Adston	1	1	1
	Morton Pinckney	1	0	1[5]+1
	Plumpton	1	0	0
	Grensnorton	2	0	0
	Blaxley	2	1	0+1
	Whitlbury & Sliveston [sic]	1	0	1
		10	3[6]	5[7]

¹ Altered from " 2 " ⁴ Altered from " 12 " ⁷ Altered from " 7 "
² Altered from " 0 " ⁵ Altered from " 2 "
³ Altered from " 8 " ⁶ Altered from " 1 "

[Hundreds]	[Townes]	[Corslettes]	[Muskettes]	[Calivers]
TOCESTRE	Teffeild	1	0	0
	Tocester and Burcot	2	0	3
	Caldecot	1	0	0+1
	Pateshall cum membris	1	1	1
	Cold Higham cum Grim[scote]	1	0	0+1
	Abthorp cum Fostres [Booth]	1	0	0
	Gaiton	1	0	1
		8	1	5

[Hundreds]	[Townes]	[Corslettes]	[Muskettes]	[Calivers]
SUTTON	Warkworth	1	0	1
	Thenford	0	0	1
	Ayno	2	2	0
	Marston La[urence]	1	0	0
	Myd[dleton] Cheny	1	1	0+1
	Culworth	1	0	1
	Chacomb	1	0	0
	Thorp Mund[eville]	1	0	0
	Farthingo	1	0	0
	Newbot[tle] cum membris	1	1	0
	Brackley	2[1]	0	2[2]+1
	Croughton	1	0	0
	Whitfield and Rodson	1	0	1+1
	Helmedon	1	0	1[3]
	Sutton Regis	2	1	0+1
	Siersham	0[4]	0	1
	Eevenly	0	0	1
	Hinton and Steane	1	0	0
	Wapnam	1	0	1
		19	5[5]	10

[Hundreds]	[Townes]	[Corslettes]	[Muskettes]	[Calivers]
CLEYLIE	Hartwell	1	0	1
	Estneston and Hulcot	1	0	0
	Paulerspery and Hethecot	2	0	0
	Covesgrav	1	0	1
	Pottspury	1	1	0
	Yardley	1	0	1
	Passenham & Denshanger	1	1	0

[1] Altered from " 3 "   [3] Altered from " 2 "   [5] Altered from " 4 "
[2] Altered from " 3 "   [4] Altered from " 1 "

[Hundreds]	[Townes]	[Corslettes]	[Muskettes]	[Calivers]
	Stoke and Shu[tlanger]	1	0	1
	Road	1	1	0
	Ashton	1	0	1[1]
	Wickens	1	0	1
	Aldrington	1	0	1
	Grafton	0	0	1
	Furtho	0	0	0
		12 [sic]	3	8
	VILLA NORTHAMPTON	4	10	6

[Scribbled on the same page]

		22	5	18
		20	5	14
		9	3	6
22	23	17	4	15
22[2]	19	12	4	7
9	9	17	3	10
17	19	10	3	5
12	11	8	1	5
82[3]	81	19	5	10
		12	3	8
		4	10	6
		150 .	46 .	104

[Total:] 300[4]

98. [fo. 166a] [TRAINED BANDS IN THE WEST DIVISION. October, 1614.]

[Enclosed with No. 96]

A liste of the foot companyes and troop of horse trayned the [blank] of October, 1614, for the tenne hundreds in the West Devision of the Covntye of Northampton, with the names of the hundreds, townes and trayned soldiers, together with their armes, and vnder the commavnde of Captain Sir Jhon Ovselye and Captaine Bellesys.

[Scribbled on this page:-] Bell: Cox 92, Butty 60 (altered to " 70 "). [John Bunche[d]] Cley[ley] Passenham 1 Ashton 1.

[1] Altered from " 2 "
[2] Altered from " 20 "
[3] Altered from " 80 "
[4] The ten hundreds of the west division were required to provide equipment for 300 footmen. It is to be noted that 46 men were to be provided with muskets, which were gradually replacing calivers as the standard infantry firearms.

[*The following figures in column:*] 44, 39, 19, 35, 23, 34, 23, 13, 09, 20, 20, 79(?) [*This last figure should be 279.*][1]

---

[1] These are evidently the numbers of trained and equipped footmen in the ten hundreds and the town of Northampton. If the order followed is the same as that in **97**, it appears that the numbers furnished by the individual hundreds were similar to those furnished in 1613—with the exception of Sutton, where the number has apparently fallen from 34 to 9.

APPENDICES

1. [DRAFT LETTER. THE COUNCIL TO THE MUSTER COMMISSIONERS IN NORTHAMPTONSHIRE. April, 1581.][1]

After our harty commendacions. We haue receiued your letters in awnswer to others of ours written before vnto you, touching musters of horsemen and provisions of horses and furniture within that County of Northampton. We perceiue by your said letters that the newe rate sett downe by the Lordes here Commissioners in that behalf from her Majestie and sent vnto you with our former letters is misliked in the contrye as a thing they are not well able to beare. Wherin we haue thought good to signifye to you that that rate was sett downe heere by good and deliberate advise, the state and abilitie of the contry being very well knowne and considered of before; which maketh vs not a litle to mervell and withall to be verie sory that of all the sheers of England we should receiue from you only this kind of awnswer: for not one hath so awnswered but you, though some, for want of the like ability and for their abilityes being perhaps more hardly rated then you, might haue had more probable cause to make such awnswere. We would be loth her Majestye should be made acquainted therewith, for we knowe her Highnes can not take it in good parte. But since your contry is very well able to beare it, as we knowe it is, and the seruice is so necessarye and commodious for the present state, we do eftsoones require you that, according to our formour letters and the said newe rate, you do forthwith proceede to the advauncement of the said service [saving yf in some fewe you shall not fynde their abilities aunswerable, which we leave to be considered of by your discrecions[1]] and with all the speed that may be to send vs a perfect certifycate of your doinges therin, suche as we may shewe vnto her Majestie, who doth often and ernestly call vppon vs for it [and will have no longer delaye nor dalying therein.[i]] And so we bid you farwell. From the Court, the [*blank*] of Aprill, 1581.

Your loving frendes.

Aprill, 1581

Copye to the Commissioners of Northamptonshyre in aunswere of their letters refusing the newe rate.

[1] P.R.O. SP 12/148/59.

2. [LETTER. KNIGHTLEY AND MONTAGU TO HATTON. 28 October, 1587.][1]

Oure duties humble remembred to your good Lordship. The xj[th] of October we receved your honorable letters, together with letters from the Lordes of her Majesties most honorable Privie Councell directed to your Lordship,[2] for putting the forces of this Countie in redines without delaye. And for the more expedicion and ease of the Country, we devided our selves and [have] taken musters in seuerall places in our hundreds; wher we have seen furnished with corsletes and calivers the number of vj[c] able men, videlicet: iij[c] armed pikes and iij[c] shott. The xxvij[th] of October we weer at Northampton and Ketheringe for the vewe of the horsemen, wher was allso Mr. Griffen and Mr. Sanders, verie willing and redy to take the charge vpon them; vnder whose ledinge we have apointed and sett downe the names of those gentlemen that shall furnishe the number of one C horse, viz. for Mr. Griffen L horses and for Mr. Sanders L horse, wherof to eche of them x dimilances and xl[tie] light horse, armed with corslettes and pistolls, beinge not muche inferior to launces. And then we had the sight of som of them, not yet all so fully furnished as is promised by the gentlemen they shalbe with speed. Suche captens as your Lordship apointed for leadinge the footemen, we finde Mr. Burnabey and Mr. Knowles verie redye; Mr Chitwood nowe dwelling in Buckinghamshier; and for Mr. Browne, Mr. Pikeringe and Mr. Nicolls, we are informed [they] be nowe at London, so that as yet we have receved no directe answer from them of their willingnes. *Yf yt please your good Lordship that we may call the noble men nowe resiant in our Cownty, namely the Lord Mordant and the Lord Compton, whom we finde willinge to joyne with vs, then shall our Country be better furnished with horsmen.*[3] We trust your Lordship will allowe of this our certificatt and willingnes of our Country, the rather for that this yeere ther hathe ben sett furthe out of our Countye ij[c] men vnder the leadinge of George Nowell, gent. And what your Lordshippes plesure is furder herin to comand vs, we are redy to perform the same accordinge to our duties, as knowethe the Almighty, who graunt to your good Lordship longe lief with encrease of honour. From Northampton, this xxviij[th] daie of October, 1587.

Your Lordshippes most humble to command,

"RI: KNYGHTLEY"
"E. MOUNTAGU"

To the Right Honorable Sir Christoffer Hatton, knight, Lord Chauncellor of England, our verie good Lord, theese.

[*Endorsement in another hand:*] November, 1587. The certificat of the Deputie Leiftenauntes in the Countie of Northampton, the first of November, 1587.

[1] P.R.O. SP 12/204/49.
[2] See **46** and **47**. In fact they received the letters on 13 October.
[3] Underlined in MS.

[*Further endorsement in yet another hand:*] No mention of any nomber of the hable men or how they are furnished. Only *100*[1] men putt vnder captans to be trayned: 20 lances, 80 light horse.

[1] Underlined in MS.

3. [LETTER. MONTAGU TO HATTON. 4 March, 1589/90.][1]
[*Holograph*]

My humble duty remembred to your good Lordship. It may please you to vnderstand that acordinge to your Honors commaundement and the dyrections from the Lordes of her Majesties moste honorable Pryuie Counsell, I haue taken a generall vewe of the old trayned bandes of horsmen and footemen, with theire armor, furniture and weapons, thorow the wholl Countye,[2] and fynishedd the same at Toster the xxvj[th] of Februarie laste. Wheare I fynde trayned soldiers that laste serued remayninge within the saide Countye to the number of iiij[c], and with the lykynge and choyse of the captains haue made supply of such as inhabit in the seuerall townes wythin theire chardge, beinge the hableste and comlyest men of person, to the number of vj[c]. And also I finde by vewe corslettes iij[c], muskettes iiij[xx], caliuers ij[c]xl[t]; all which make the number of vj[c] armor and shott to arme and furnish the former forces of this County, as heretoffore hath beene certefied. The bandes of the horsmen that your Honor hath commaundedd by your honorable letters to bee vnder the leadinge of Mr. Saunders and Mr. Parre Lane (who haue beene with mee at Ketheringe and Northampton and taken the vewe of them) will hardlie fall owte to bee furnishedd with the number of l[t] in theire seuerall leadinges, by reason that theire are divers gentlemen deade, some that haue lefte the Cuntrie and others that bee not chargable, by reason of theyre offices of sheriffweeke: which amounteth neare the number of xx[t] horse, as by a note here inclosed may apeare,[3] and will not bee supplied by such gentlemen as are now remyninge in the Countye.

And wheare by theire Lordshippes letters theire pleasures are that this County should bee charged withe proporcion of j laste of powder and fyve hundred waighte of match: I would gladlie know whether it stande better with your Honors lykinge to have the Cuntry charged and to make presente payment for the same, or ells that proporcion to bee prouidedd in the markett townes by the chapmen at reasonable prices and to haue it allwaies in redines, as by a proporcion of euery markett towne may likewise apeare vnto your Honor.[4] I haue receaued your honorable letters in the beehalf of my neighbour Gibbes, but as yet I finde noe occasion nether place of seruice to imploy him in.

Thus restinge in this, as in all other, at your honorable direction, I comend your good Lordship to the gouerment of the Almightye, who graunte to you longe lyffe wyth health. Boughton, this iiij[th] of March, 1589.

Your good Lordshippes and at commandement,

E. MOUNTAGU

To the Righte Honorable Sir Christopher Hatton, of the noble Order of the Garter, knightt, Lorde Chauncellor of England,

[1] P.R.O. SP 12/231/10.
[2] Since Knightley was still in disgrace, Montagu at this time seems to have had sole responsibility for the militia in both parts of the shire.
[3] See Appendix 4.
[4] See Appendix 5.

Lord Lewtenaunte of her Highnes County of Northampton and one of her Majesties moste honorable Priuy Councell, my verie good lorde, theise.

[*Endorsement in another hand:*] 4 Marche, 1589. From Sir Edward Mountague, Deputie Lieutennant for Northamptonshire. Certificat of musters for that Countye. Whether the pouther to be prouided by the townes shalbe bought at the charg of the townes and Contry, or whether [chapmen*ᵃ*] it may not suffice to haue the chapmen of the townes to haue the proportion in redines to issue forth to the Contry.

4. [Persons Dead, Gone or not Chargeable. 4 March, 1589/90][1]

[Enclosed with App. 3]

Comitatus Northampton. A note of such persons as bee deade and are gone out of the Countie, beinge charged wyth the fynding of dymylaunces and light horse, together with those that are not chargable by reason of their offices of sheriffeswycke.[2]

		Dymilaunces	Light horse	
Deade	Sir Robarte Lane, knight	j	j	
	Mr. Worme		j	
	Mr. Ashbie		j	
	Mr. Haslewood	j		
	Mr. Dalison		j	
Haue lefte the Countie	The Ladie St. John	j	j	In toto xix^t
	Sir William Fitzwilliams	j		
	Mr. Anthony Mildmay	j	ij	
	Mr. Sherley	j	ij	
Not chargable by reason of theire offyces	Sir George Farmor, knighte, Sheryffe	j	j	
	Mr. Clarke, Sheriffe of Oxeffordeshire	j	j	

[In toto xix^t ^d]

[1] P.R.O. SP 12/231/10(i). In Montagu's hand.
[2] Cf. **62**.

5. A NOTE OF THE PROPORCION OF POWDER AND MACH IN THE SEUERALL MARKET TOWNES WITHIN THE COUNTIE OF NORTHAMPTON. [4 March, 1589/90.][1]

[Enclosed with App. 3]

	Weighte	Weight	
Peterborow powder:			
barrels ij, contayning	ij^c	mach	*li.*
Oundell powder:			
barrells j, contayning	j^c	mach	*li.*
Wellingborow powder:			
barrells j, contayning	j^c	mach	*li.*
Ketheringe powder:			
barrells j, contayning	j^c	mach	*li.*
Higham Ferrers, Rothwell and Thrapston:			
barrells j, contayning	j^c	mach	*li.*
Northampton powder:			
barrells iiij, contayning	iiij^c	mach j^c*li.*	
Daventry powder:			
barrells j, contayning	j^c	mach	*li.*
Toster cum Brackley:			
barrells j, contayning	j^c	mach	*li.*

In toto:
contayning xij^c
barrells xij,
pounde.
In toto:
mach
v^c weighte

---

[1] P.R.O. SP 12/231/10(i). In Montagu's hand. It is to be noted that only Northampton appears to be charged with the provision of a fixed quantity of match. Cf. the list in **20** and **22**.

GLOSSARY

Bill	Halberd.
Caliver	Infantry handgun, about $3\frac{1}{2}$ feet long, fired without a rest.
Cornet	Junior cavalry officer, who carried the standard.
Coronell	Colonel.
Corslet	Armour (and often all other necessary equipment) for a pikeman.
Demi-lance	Cavalryman with heavy armour.
Halberd	Military weapon—combination of spear and battle-axe.
Light horseman	Cavalryman with light armour.
Oath of Supremacy	Oath of allegiance to the Queen as Supreme Governor of the Church of England.
Petronel	Cavalry pistol.
Posse Comitatus	The whole able-bodied manpower of the shire, traditionally called up by the sheriff in the event of invasion or insurrection, but of little practical significance in Elizabethan times.
Provost Marshal	Officer appointed to punish (by martial law) disorderly persons, both civil and military, in times of emergency.
Quorum	Certain selected J.P.s, whose presence was necessary to constitute a bench. By the 1580s the great majority of J.P.s were " of the quorum ".
Roundel, rundell	A circular target, used in shooting practice.
Shott	Men equipped with firearms.

INDEX OF PERSONS AND PLACES

* Indicates that the name occurs more than once on a page.

Creswell, Croswell, Robert, 83; Thomas, 74, 78, 80, 83; ———, 45.

Crick, 88.

Crisp, Crispe, Augustine, 6, 44.

Croft, Crofte, Sir James, 17, 30, 41, 48.

Cromer, William, 11.

Crosby, Crosborowe, Thomas, 65.

Cross, Crosse, William, 28.

Croughton, 91.

Culworth, 23, 91.

Cumberland (George Clifford), Earl of, 33.

Curtis, Curtice, Giles, 65; Henry, 65; Richard, 74.

Dallington, 89.

Dallison, Dalison, Edward, 5, 100.

Danby, Danbie, William, 28.

Danford, J., 64.

Danvers, Davers, Samuel, 6, 20, 44, 83.

Darby, Darbie, Thomas, 64; Wilfred, 64.

Darling, Darlinge, Thomas, 64.

Daventry, Daventre, Daventrye, xxiv, 12, 19*, 21, 23, 28, 67, 88, 101.

Davison, William, 17, 26, 32, 33.

Davy, Davye, Simon, 64.

Dawes, Nicholas, 65; Owen, 65.

Dawson, Dawsone, Richard, 64.

Delapré Abbey, xiv, 88.

Denshanger, 91.

Denton, 90.

Derby (Henry Stanley), Earl of, 17, 25, 33*, 35, 43, 48, 70.

Dexter, Henry, 64.

Dillingham, William, 64.

Dobbs, Dobbes, Thomas, 64.

Dodford, 88.

Dombleston, John, 28.

Dormer, Darmor, Dormar, Dormor, William, 6, 21*, 44, 83.

Dorne, see Thorne.

Doulton, Doltone, Nicholas, 64.

Dover, 11, 13.

Dowse, Henry, 65.

Drake, Sir Francis, xxiii.

Drawater, Richard, 65.

Drayton (Middx.), 84.

Dredwaye, Francis, 64.

Drury, Drewerie, Drurye, Sir Drue, 34; Henry, 65.

Dryden, Dredon, Dreidon, Drydon, Erasmus, 44; George, 45; John, 6.

Duddington, Dodington, 12, 19*.

Dudley, Edward, 5; William, 20.

Dunmore, Thomas, 65.

Dunstable (Beds.), xxiv.

Duston, 89.

Dykes, Edmund, 65.

Eales, Edmund, 65.

East Haddon, 89.

Easton, Eston, J., 64; William, 74.

Easton Neston, Estneston, 91.

Eastwick, Nicholas, 65.

Eaton, Eton, Laurence, 74, 78, 80.

Eccles, Eckles, Thomas, 64.

Ecton, 19, 20.

Edgcote, Edgcot, 89.

Ekins, Eakins, Eakyns, Richard, 65; Thomas, 65.

Elmely, see Evenley.

Elms, Elmes, Edmund, 4; John, 21*.

Elsey, Richard, 28.

Ely Place, Holborn, xxxi, 62.

Emley, Emeley, Emely, Thomas, 44, 79.

Emmerson, William, 67.

Engille, W., 65.

Essex, xxix, xxxi and n.

Essex (Robert Devereux), Earl of, xxx.

Eustace, Wstis, John, 74.

Evenley, Eevenly, Elmely, Elmnely, 32, 33*, 91.

Everdon, Everdons, 88.

Every, Everie, Robert, 64.

Exeter, Earl of, see Cecil, Sir Thomas.

Eydon, 89.

Eyre, Ere, Thomas, 79.

Fane, Sir Thomas, 10; Thomas, 10, 11.

Farthingoe, Farthingo, 91.

Farthingstone, Farthingston, 79, 88.

Faversham (Kent), 13.

Fawsley, Faulesly, Fawesley, hundred of, 23, 24, 66, 78, 79, 88.

Fermor, Farmar, Farmer, Farmor, Sir George, xviii, xxvii, xxix and n, xxxiin, xxxiii, 6, 20, 44, 83, 84, 85, 100; Jerome, 6, 20, 44.

Finch, Fynche, Erasmus, 11.

Firmin, Ferman, J., 64.

Fisher, Fysher, Fyssher, George, 64; Peter, 64; Robert, 28; Thomas, 65*.

Fitzwilliam, Fitzwilliams, Fytzwilliam, Sir William, 4, 20, 100.

Fleming, Captain, xxiii.

Fletcher, J., 64.

Flore, Flower, 89.

Folkestone, 11, 13.

Fordwich (Kent), 13.

Fosbrook, Fosbroke, John, 5.

Foster, Edmund, 73.

Foster's Booth, Fostres Booth, 91.

Fotheringhay, Fodringey, Fothryngaye, xvii, 22, 23, 33.

Fox, Foxe, George, 28; Richard, 6, 44, 79.

Foxley, Foxeley, Foxely, Francis, 6, 44, 83.

France, xxx.

Francis, Frauncis, Edward, 64.

Freeman, Freman, John, 44.

Frere, Freear, Thomas, 73, 78.

Frisby, Frisbie, Frysbie, Henry, 64; Humphrey, 64.

Mildmay, Mildmaye, Sir Anthony, xxxiii, 100; Sir Walter, xvi, xviii, 20, 21, 24, 26, 27, 29, 54, 70, 71*.
Miles, Myles, Laurence, 64; Maurice, 44, 74, 78, 80; Richard, 64.
Milton, 90.
Milton Regis, Myddelston (Kent), 11, 13.
Mitchell, Mychell, ——, 48.
Montagu, Montague, Montigew, Moun-tagu, Mountague, Sir Edward (d.1602), xii, xvii-xxx, xxxii, xxiiin, 2, 4, 15-16, 25-27, 30, 34*, 37-42, 46-49, 51-60, 62, 67-69, 72-77, 80-86, 96, 98-99, 100n, 101n; Sir Edward (later Lord Montagu of Boughton), xxii, xxxiii, 21*, 39.
Moore, Moorye, Edward, 65.
Mordaunt, Lewis, Lord, xviii, xx, 7, 20, 21, 96.
Moreton Pinkney, Moreton Pinckney, 84, 90.
Morgan, Anthony, 5, 45, 83; Bartholo-mew, 63; Thomas, 44.
Morris, Mores, Hugh, 28.
Mortimer, Mortymer, Thomas, 64.
Morton, Moreton, Lieutenant, 66.
Mosby, Mosbye, Richard, 64.
Moulshoe, Mulsho, Thomas, 5.
Moulton, 90.
Mounsteven, Mountstevinge, John, 5.
Mumford, Thomas, 65.
Muscot, Anthony, 5.

Nantwich (Cheshire), 28.
Naseby, Navesby, 89.
Nassaburgh, Nassaburghe, hundred of, xxxi, 38. See also Peterborough, soke of.
Neale, John, 5, 45, 83.
Nelson, Nellson, John, 28.
Netherlands, xxi, xxviii, xxix and n, 39, 40.
Newbone, W., 64.
Newbottle, Newbotle, Nobottell, 91.
Newbottle Grove, Nobottle Grove, hun-dred of, 23*, 66, 78, 79, 89.
Newnham, 88.
Nicolls, Niccolles, Nicholes, Francis, xxii*, xxiii, xxiv, 5, 62 and n, 63*, 65, 96; William, 20.
Nobottle, see Newbottle.
Norfolk, xxxi.
Northampton, xvi, xix, xxiv, xxix, 21, 23, 24, 25-29, 66, 67, 78, 79, 92, 93n, 96*, 98, 101*.
Northampton (Henry Howard), Earl of, 25.
Northampton (William Parr), Marquess of, xviii and n, xxvii, xxxiii.
Northamptonshire, east division, xiv and n, xv, xix, xxiv and n, xxvi, xxix, 4, 39, 63, 67, 82; west division, xiii, xiv and n, xv, xviiin, xix-xxi, xxiv, xxvi, xxxiii.

xxxiv, 5, 23, 39, 44, 65, 78-79, 82, 88, 91.
Norton, xxxiii, 88.
Norton, hundred of, see Greens Norton, hundred of
Norton, John, 5.
Norwich, Norwiche, Simon, 4.
Nowell, George, 39, 96.
Nutt, William, 28.

Odell, Odill, Fulk, 6, 44, 79.
Oldman, Anthony, 28.
Onley, Only, 88.
Onley, Onley, Onlie, Edward, 6, 20, 45; Thomas, 74, 78, 79, and n.
Orginer, Thomas, 64.
Orme, Humphrey, 5.
Osborne, John, 4.
Osnam, George, 65.
Oundle, Ondell, Oundell, xxiv, 21, 75, 101.
Ouseley, Ouselye, Sir John, 92.
Overstone, Overston, 90.
Oxfordshire, xvii, 100.

Pack, Packe, Henry, 65; Thomas, 65.
Page, J., 65.
Painter, Paynter, William, 73, 78, 80.
Palmer, Henry, 11*, Maurice, 74; Thomas, 74; William, 20; W., 64.
Pargeter, Pargiter, Robert, 44; William, 6.
Paris, Parrys, Henry, see Taylor alias Paris.
Parker, Nicholas, 28; Robert, 28.
Parma, Duke of, xxiii, 60.
Passenham, 91, 92.
Pattishall, Pateshall, 91.
Paulerspury, 91.
Paulet, Poulet, Sir Amias, 34*, 48, 70.
Peabody, Paybodie, J., 65.
Peacham, J., 65.
Peake, Edward, 64.
Pedder, Henry, 33.
Pee, John, 73.
Pemberton, Pemarton, 24.
Pembroke (Henry Herbert), Earl of, 33.
Penn, Pen, J., 64.
Penney, Penny, Brian, 75.
Peter, Nicholas, 64.
Peterborough, Peterborow, Peterbor-owghe, Peterbrough, Peterbrughe, 21, 75, 101; soke of, xxiv, 38, 64. See also Nassaburgh, hundred of.
Peterborough, Bishop of, xxivn, 20, 21.
Pevensey (Sussex), 13.
Phipps, Phippes, Thomas, 64.
Pickering, Pickeringe, Pyckeryng, Pycker-ynge, Boniface, 5; Gilbert, xxii, 20, 21*, 39, 96; John, 5, 20; J., 64.
Piddington, 75, 90.
Pitman, Pytman, Peter, 28.
Pitsford, Pisford, 90.

INDEX OF SUBJECTS